In praise of

FLYING SPIRIT
A LEADER'S GUIDE TO
CREATING GREAT ORGANIZATIONS

"What I like best is the book's solid foundation of values, backed up by the practical advice you would expect from someone who has been there — one of the most inspiring leaders I have ever worked for."

General Merrill A. McPeak, U.S.A.F. (Ret.)****
Chief of U.S. Air Force 1990-1994

"Those who aspire to be leaders should read FLYING SPIRIT. I highly recommend this book to newcomers for learning what makes a great leader and to experienced people in the field as a reminder of how to facilitate people becoming productive leaders."

Margaret Hartzler, Ph.D., President of Type Resources
Consultants and Professional Trainers
in the Myers-Briggs Type Indicator®

"Drawn from the mind and heart of a true war hero, FLYING SPIRIT teaches solid, synergistic principles of leadership in a compelling, easy-to-read manner. A tremendous addition to any personal library."

Dr. Stephen Covey
Author of The Seven Habits of Highly Effective People

"FLYING SPIRIT is the sky writing of a true ace, a man I have admired and followed for over 20 years, a friend whose smile makes small children draw near and a warrior whose frown you'd hope to never see. Many people talk about ALIGNMENT, but Hal Shook shows you what it is."

Will Reed, Translator and Journalist
for the Japanese Automotive Industry,
Author: Three books on Ki-Akido/Japanese Culture

"A great book for making you THINK, BELIEVE, DREAM and DARE."
Mike Vance
Former Dean, Disney University
Chairman, Creative Thinking Association of America
Co-author of Think Out of the Box **and** Break Out of the Box

"This book is great! I read it on a plane, sitting on the edge of my seat. It was such a surprise to me that military experiences could apply to business. But after all, the bottom line in the military is life or death. In business you either live or die too, based on the decisions you make."
Edward "Beau" Necco, Director, Ed Necco Associates,
Human Resource Consultants, Huntington, West Virginia

"Hal Shook understands leadership and is a superb teacher. In FLYING SPIRIT he's a coach, a mentor, a cheerleader and a guide to find and nurture the leader that lurks somewhere in all of us."
Margaret Dunkle, Director, IEL Policy Exchange,
The Institution for Educational Leadership, Inc.

"Hal Shook is a hero, and FLYING SPIRIT is the first management and leadership book I could not put down. His stories make his principles come to life."
Sig Hutchinson, President, Sig Hutchinson and Associates,
Raleigh, North Carolina

"Should be required reading for every family, business, corporation, etc., etc. EXCEL-LENT!"
Bonnie Gilewicz, Mother of 8, Teacher, Cary, North Carolina

"Readers of Hal Shook's FLYING SPIRIT will gain a powerful and practical tool for building their own leadership abilities and the organizations they run."
Ronald E. Guzik, Vice President, United Financial, Inc.,
Naperville, Illinois, author of The Inner Game of
Entrepreneuring **(forthcoming)**

"FLYING SPIRIT is a common sense game plan for success. It is founded on a value drawn approach for your business and personal life."
Terry Stoneman, President, Zipcom, Inc.,
Cary, North Carolina

FLYING SPIRIT

FLYING SPIRIT

A Leader's Guide to Creating
Great Organizations

Hal Shook, Col., U.S.A.F. (Ret.)
with Allen Overmyer

Foreword by Robert Nideffer

HUMANOMICS
PUBLISHING

Systems where People Matter

FLYING SPIRIT

Library of Congress Number: 98-73357
ISBN (Hardbound): 0-9666085-0-X
ISBN (Softbound): 0-9666085-1-8

Editorial Coordination: John Patrick Grace
Grace Associates, Ltd., at Publishers Place, Inc.
P.O. Box 2395
Huntington, West Virginia 25724

Cover and Book Design: Mark S. Phillips
Marketing+Design Group
Point Pleasant • Huntington, West Virginia

First Edition
First Printing, August 1998
Second Printing, April 1999

Printed in Canada

945 Fourth Avenue, Suite 200A
Huntington, West Virginia 25701

Dedicated to the members
of the 506th Fighter Squadron
January through October 1944

Myrtle Beach, South Carolina
Winkton, England
Normandy, France, A-5
Bretigny (Paris), A-48
Juvincourt (Reims), A-68
St. Trond, Belgium, A-92

Until we meet again,
may God hold you in the palm of His hand.

— Old Irish Blessing

TABLE OF CONTENTS

CHAPTER THREE

CHAPTER FOUR

CHAPTER FIVE

CHAPTER SIX

CHAPTER SEVEN

CHAPTER EIGHT

CHAPTER ELEVEN

CHAPTER TWELVE

CHAPTER THIRTEEN

THE RESTLESS QUEST FOR CONTINUING IMPROVEMENT

CHAPTER FOURTEEN

HOLDING ON TO SUCCESS

FOREWORD

Hal Shook is one of those rare individuals who actually practices what he preaches, twenty-four hours a day, 365 days a year. I've seen him talk to "shakers and breakers," and I've seen him talk to minimum wage earners. What never changes is his obvious respect for the individual and his affirmation of their worth. Hal makes every person with whom he comes into contact feel valued and important. To me he is a role model, someone whose standards and beliefs I would one day hope to live up to.

I must confess that when Hal told me he was writing this book, I had some serious doubts about it. I wasn't sure about his ability to make the bridge between his experiences as a leader in World War II and those of the leaders of today. However, as I've watched the book evolve, I've concluded that the lessons he has to offer are truly timeless. Even in the flying examples, he speaks directly to the excitement and urgency I see in today's highly competitive business world.

While this book is about leadership and management, it is also about something deeper and more fundamental than mechanics or techniques. Hal draws on his own experience in combat and throughout a lifetime of leadership to clarify what lies at the heart of all great performance, whether it be individual or group. He speaks compellingly about the importance of having a mission, identifying core values, and defining a specific objective. More importantly, he delves into the intangible quality that underlies a winning effort and binds all of its components together. Hal points out that it is a set of core beliefs that provides each of us with the will to carry on when things seem overwhelming and totally out of control. This quality can be expressed as "spirit," which gives us or our team that drive, synergy, and extra push to win.

Like Hal, I've run into times when I didn't have the answers, nor did I believe in my own ability to get the job done. At those times, however, it was a sense of mission, an obligation to others, that kept me from giving up and forced me to look beyond myself and my immediate circumstances. Ultimately, it was my belief in that mission which allowed me to perform in the face of what seemed to be overwhelming odds.

Over the past twenty years, I've had the opportunity to work with elite level performers in business and sports, both from an applied perspective and as a research scientist. I've seen the lessons of leadership, teamwork, and productivity that are taught in this book played out again and again. I know that winning takes tremendous effort and concentration, and that it also takes a lot of heart. In today's highly competitive climate, it isn't technical or tactical weaknesses that separate winners from losers in the boardroom or on the playing field. Instead, it's a breakdown in interpersonal relationships and/or a loss of faith in one's own ability and the ability of the team, that leads to failure.

Hal Shook believes that his mission in life is to affirm the value and worth of other human beings. This mission and the beliefs that support it have given him the courage to perform with grace under fire. Hal does not pretend to have all the answers, but I believe that his book gives us a greater understanding of what makes good into great, for ourselves and for our team. If we can truly hear what he has to say, perhaps each of us may find some guidelines that will not fail us, no matter what.

Robert Nideffer, Ph.D.

Dr. Robert Nideffer has published more than ten books and a hundred articles related to attention or concentration and performance. One of the world's leading sports psychologists, he has worked with elite and professional athletes worldwide and with the 1984 and 1988 U.S. Olympic Track and Field Teams. Dr. Nideffer also has provided performance enhancement programs to business executives and managers at all levels.

HIGH FLIGHT

Oh, I have slipped the surly bonds of earth
and danced the skies on laughter-silvered wings;
sunward I've climbed, and joined the tumbling mirth
of sun-split clouds — and done a hundred things
you have not dreamed of — wheeled and soared and swung
high in the sunlit silence. Hov'ring there,
I've chased the shouting wind along, and flung
my eager craft through footless halls of air.

Up, up the long delirious, burning blue
I have topped the wind swept heights with easy grace
where never lark, or even eagles flew.
And, while with silent, lifting mind I've trod
the high untrespassed sanctity of space,
put out my hand, and touched the face of God.

John Gillispie Magee, Jr.

FLYING SPIRIT

CHAPTER

VALUING PEOPLE

Anyone who doesn't get along with people has earned the kiss of death...
because all we have around here are people.
Lee Iacocca

Bedrock for Building a Great Organization

Over the years I have been intrigued by why some companies succeed and others fail — even though they start on a similar basis, with bright dreams, fine ideas, and excellent people. But some outfits just don't take off, or they soon find themselves in a rut, going nowhere. In other organizations, something seems to click, and somehow they take wing and soar.

You can tell the difference as soon as you walk in the door. It's in the eyes of the people who greet you. In a dynamic organization, you can see it in smiles and hear it in laughter. There's a spirit of enthusiasm in the air. In the outfit that gets stuck along the way, you get a different feeling. You see long faces, you hear grumbling, and you have a sense of wasted time. The message is: "I don't want to be here." People are tied down in their resourcefulness and initiative, maybe keeping a low profile to avoid criticism — the only feedback they get.

Both organizations have a definite identity and spirit. One is positive, with people inspired by a sense of mission and purpose. The other is negative. People are just getting by. What is it that makes the difference?

Without fail, I have found that a highly charged organization, reaching its full potential, is operating from the basis of a rock-solid inner core. The core is made up of what, to me, life is all about: *people, values, and relationships.* People are the basis of everything else. Values are what define and give our lives direction. Relationships are the means through which we interact with our world. The first and most important element is *people.*

The Primary Resource

In the coal mines of Scranton, Pennsylvania, immigration of the 19th century fed a virtual wage-slavery culture in which workers labored twelve to fourteen hours a day to meet their quota, sometimes hacking anthracite coal from a vein so narrow they could not stand up. Their housing, tools, and even the dynamite and fuses they used were deducted from their wages; they were permanently in debt to the company. To feed the family, their children would go into the mines at age twelve, and with no eduction, could seldom escape. Many were killed in accidents. If a man died, his body was dumped at his widow's front door, and she was given notice to vacate.

Workers were cogs in a machine. They had nothing in common with the company that employed them. It was "us" against "them," a relationship of subdued guerrilla warfare.

The structure of our world has changed dramatically since that time, and with it, the nature of the workplace. The concept of workers as interchangeable parts has evolved into honoring people as the company's most valuable resource.

Winning in the highly competitive and technologically sophisticated environment of today requires a relationship of people working together in a spirit of cooperation and teamwork. In a great organization, people share the values of the company and own its mission and objectives as their own. They are in many ways the true owners, and they have a sense of joy in being there. They like what they do, and they're proud of it.

In turn, the company honors them for a practical, bottom-line reason. Their minds, their creativity, and their ability to innovate are the real capital of the organization.

Today industry widely acknowledges the fact that people are its primary resource, and that this valuable resource must be nurtured and honored for the good of the organization. Everybody knows that. Right?

Why, then, are so many people miserable in the workplace?

Managers, of necessity, tend to be product-oriented. Their task is to get the job done. Focusing on goals, objectives, accountability and time schedules, they tend to overlook the people side, upon which the attainment of everything else depends. Goals and objectives are only achieved through people.

Products may become obsolete before they even fully enter the marketplace, such as Japan's analog high definition television system. It is the ability to innovate that counts, and innovation depends upon people. The point here is not simply to create and produce a product or service. Rather, it is to build the kind of organization that will sustain creativity and innovation and provide the highest levels of consumer satisfaction on a long-term basis.

John Naisbitt, of *Megatrends*, has seen that the layoffs and cutbacks of recent times have sapped worker morale, making it difficult for a company to rebuild on a sound basis. He says the result is "a rising awareness that happy workers — not technology, not TQM, not cutthroat competition — may be the key to success." He predicts:

As technology and other strategic tools become easier to acquire, worker-friendly employers will outperform their more profit-minded competitors by growing margins.[1]

The most competitive companies of the future will draw upon a workforce of people who are respected by the company and who find satisfaction and commitment in their work. The great strength of the American workforce is its inventiveness and creativity. Releasing this creativity through honoring the individual and making him or her care is playing to our strong suit.

It all comes back to us, the good and the bad. We reap what we sow. People respond in kind. Treat them with compassion and understanding and they respond accordingly. "Treat people right and they treat you right" is another expression of the Golden Rule.

As my father used to tell me, "Kill 'em with kindness, kid."

1. THE RIGHT PEOPLE

The first step in building the foundation is to select the right people. This begins with knowing exactly what you need. What are your requirements? What are you trying to do? What do you want this person to do? The initial and key step is the *job analysis*.

In fitting the person to the job, skills and experience are clearly essential criteria, but less tangible factors such as personality, character, values, and motivation also should be weighed heavily.

Instruments such as the Myers-Briggs Type Indicator® and the Personal Profile System, among others, can be useful in pointing out how an individual might fit into the organization. Psychological profiles, however, are not a basis for hiring or rejecting a person, but only a means of surfacing issues you may want to question. For example, if someone is heavily left-brain oriented, you might want to find out how he or she gets along with people. With a right-brained person you might want to see if they can deal with a task that requires the logical connection of ideas or steps.

Your interview should include an exploration of the candidate's personal values. You could ask, "What principles do you follow in making important decisions?" Through focused questions, you can determine a person's attitude on various issues and, in general, what is important to him or her in life.

If people complain of unfair treatment in the past and start shooting others down, chances are good that they are not taking responsibility for their own lives. Similarly, if a person exhibits racial or ethnic bias, this too comes out of a core value system and should be a warning flag.

Sensitivity to others is an important trait. The attitude, "I'm gonna get this job done no matter what," may signal drive and determination, but it also can mean that no one else matters.

The Right Values

In interviewing prospective employees, Mike Shook, president of an award-winning computer services company, Strategic Technologies, Inc., first tries to find out "just what are the most important, rock-solid values in your life?" "What is something that is unarguable, that you just feel so firmly?" He also asks, "If you as an adult were going back to high school to address graduating seniors, what would you tell them? What are the reasons for your success and what is their value base?"

If a man says, "I have two daughters," Shook asks what four or five things the individual would tell the girls he had tried as a father to teach them. "What are four or five things you learned from your own parents? What is important in life and what is so right that you cannot argue its substance?" He says, "It all comes back to what you've learned and how you feel about what's the right thing to do."

The next phase of the values definition is to find out from the person what others would say about that person and his or her values (the person's boss, friends, customers, and peers.) In effect, Shook is asking, "Are you who you say you are?" All of these viewpoints present a coherent picture. "You know, it's funny," he says, "over an hour of discussion all those things will dovetail and will spell out what is important."

The Right Kind of Intelligence

A great organization is built on people with a high level of people skills. It isn't enough just to be competent. The person you bring into your "family" is going to have to be *compatible*. That individual will have to share your values, be able to work as part of a team, and if your corporate culture honors and respects people, the individual will have to hold others in that same high regard.

Recent psychological research indicates that this entire area of people skills may be more important to success in life than intelligence as measured by IQ tests. Dr. Daniel Goleman, in his book, *Emotional Intelligence*, says that rational intelligence alone contributes, at best, to 20 percent of our success. The other 80 percent depends upon non-IQ forces, ranging from social class to luck.[2]

The area of emotional intelligence (EI) is non-rational and cannot be measured by intelligence testing. It has to do with personality and character, our knowledge of ourselves and other people, our sensitivity to others, and our ability to discipline ourselves and control our emotions. This range of capabilities, having to do with our emotional side, is crucial to how well we do in every area of our lives. The quality of our business and personal *relationships* largely determines how effective we will be in life. In relationships, knowing ourselves and others is everything.

Emotional intelligence begins with self-awareness. From knowing and understanding our own emotions, we can control our behavior and respond to the world effectively. If you fly off the handle, you are allowing yourself to be hijacked and defeated by your own emotions. Other characteristics of EI are self-motivation, persistence and zeal, and being able to empathize with others.

People who excel in life, whose relationships are strong and positive, and who stand out in the workplace have a high degree of emotional intelligence. In a larger sense, the personal traits of self-discipline, altruism, and compassion are the keystones of our democratic society.

If I read these findings correctly, I see three main elements in EI: the need to incorporate head and heart, the application of positive thinking, and the essentiality of alignment and harmony in an organization through team interacting and networking.

Selecting the right person should always have more to do with that person's personality and character traits than with his or her pure intellectual or technical skills. Skills can be learned. Character can't.

2. TRAINING

Having selected the right people on a "whole person" basis, the next step is to ensure that they receive the right *training*. However, this is not a one-time process. Training always goes on. If you stop training, you stop growing.

Some organizations operate on a "sink or swim" principle: put someone into a job unprepared and see if he or she can bob to the surface. That makes about as much sense as a Salem witchcraft trial by water. If you survive, you'll be burned as a witch. If you drown, you're innocent. Either way, you're dead.

A highly skilled worker might suddenly be drafted into management and find that he or she has to develop a whole new range of skills. The task is now to get the job done through people. *This change in orientation should be, but seldom is, prepared for through adequate training.*

I am convinced that you can take the great majority of people, even if they are headed in the wrong direction, and turn them around through guidance and trust. I believe in a "95/5" rule. Five percent of the people in the world cause 95 percent of the problems. In the case of the five percent, you've got to hit them in the head with a two by four. Even then you're not going to get 100 percent out of them. But when you influence and persuade, you can bring the vast majority into the mission.

Industry is becoming more involved in education because the American educational system is not turning out the kind of people industry needs. And this is not just in the area of job skills. If a corporation can further develop employees' values and character, the rest can fall into place.

We Learn Best by Doing

Training is a phased process. You start with *telling* and *showing* people how you want the job done, then you watch them perform the task. They learn by doing. As they progress, they *gain confidence* in themselves. Finally, they earn your *trust*, and in your coaching and mentoring, you have earned theirs. The end result of the training cycle is to develop trust and self-confidence.

Doing develops creativity. I've found that the more I learn, in life and work, the more creative I become. First, we need to get down the routine essentials of a process. Then we can call upon our creativity to improve the process.

Soon after I arrived in England in 1944 as commander of the 506th Fighter Squadron, I flew my first combat mission as a wingman to an experienced leader. On my first mission, a four-hour flight escorting heavy bombers over Frankfurt, Germany, I had to watch helplessly as a B-24 was hit by flak and went down in flames. A few days later, I went on my first dive-bombing mission on what we called the "Bethune Bombing Range," a railroad marshaling yard in France. When I came back, I briefed all the pilots and aircrews in the squadron and passed on what I had learned.

At the end of my tour, I repeated the process with my replacement. I began with describing our responsibilities and missions, then flew with him on my wing, observing how he performed, talking with him, and debriefing him on the ground. After a few missions, I gave him a flight of four airplanes to lead and watched to see if he developed confidence and trust within the flight. Then I gave him leadership of the squadron, walking him through the ropes and keeping a close eye on his performance.

On our first combat mission together, we saw the smoke of a train engine. "Let's go get it!" I said. But then the train disappeared between two hills, and as we dove after it, the hills erupted with a murderous flak. It was a decoy! I did some quick evasive action, which meant getting the hell out of there. As a general rule, it is probably best to conduct training when your chances of getting shot down are relatively low.

3. NOURISH AND ENCOURAGE

With skillful selection and training accomplished, the next step is to *nourish growth and encourage creativity*. This is the coaching stage.

You encourage people's growth by *listening* to them and hearing them. When they come up with ideas (which you have encouraged them to do), do something about it. Take action. Create the climate in which everyone knows that "We're always looking for your ideas." Provide feedback. Make it a two-way street.

Have brainstorming sessions to harness the employees' collective ideas and energies in problem solving. If you have shown people that you have a deep and sincere interest in them as individuals, they will feel good about themselves and will be better able to open up with others. Brainstorming can produce real breakthroughs.

To encourage creativity, let people find their own solutions. At a training school I commanded to make the transition from prop-driven aircraft to jets for the Korean War, we never insisted that the student perform every maneuver exactly like his instructor. These were all experienced pilots. They knew what they were doing. The end result had to be correct, but each student could do it best in his own way.

During the check ride, it was normal practice to pull the throttle back to simulate a flame-out, which is a complete loss of engine ignition and power. But I would yank the throttle all the way back and actually flame the engine out (after I knew what the student could do). If the engine wouldn't restart, I could always glide the bird in and land it.

It was interesting to see how pilots varied in their responses. Some whistled right through and got a quick airstart. Others hesitated, unable to believe what had just happened to them, and a few lost it. But once they calmed down and I talked them through the procedure, their confidence was not only restored, but it was significantly better than before the flight.

Managers are consistently concerned with improving performance. They often overlook the essential fact that self-confidence or self-image, the *internal belief system*, is the generator of performance.

4. Empowerment

Empowerment is the point at which the manager can give up control and delegate authority and responsibility to another person. It's amazing how many outfits are reluctant to do that. They haven't developed the *trust* that would give them confidence in letting go. The inability to let go is due to a failure to train people properly and bring them along through development and encouragement. It is also due to a lack of self-confidence on the part of management.

Through the process of training, nourishing and encouraging, both the manager and the employee increase their trust in each other. As individuals' competence and self-esteem grow, the manager can gradually devolve responsibility, relying on them and allowing them to rely on themselves. At this point, the manager has to *get out of the way and let it happen.*

5. VALIDATION

We either validate or invalidate everyone we meet, every day of our lives. *Validation* means to acknowledge someone's existence and worth. It might be as simple as giving someone a smile. Invalidation can be in not hearing what a coworker has to say because our own concerns seem more important. An organization's culture will encourage or discourage validation, based upon its values and guiding principles.

• *A Deep Human Need*

All of us have a deep-seated need to be worthy in our own eyes and the eyes of the world. We gain this legitimacy partially through the roles we perform in life, personal and professional. But we cannot place the laurel wreath on our own heads, as Napoleon did in crowning himself in Notre Dame. We need some acknowledgment that we are appreciated. The message, "You matter," goes a long way in creating a positive corporate culture in which people feel good about themselves.

• *Listening and Learning*

In our heart of hearts, each of us knows that the most fascinating subject in the world is *me*. Many people interact with others strictly on that basis. That's why it's so hard to hear what someone else has to say. We also practice selective hearing, which is to hear what we want to hear and tune out the rest. Listening requires an interchange with another person in which we hear what is being said, acknowledge it, and in some way respond to it.

• *Sharing Information*

Keeping people in the dark and opening the door now and then to dump in a bucket of manure is a good way to grow mushrooms, but it doesn't do much for group synergy. Information is power. Sharing information is a way of saying "you are trusted," but it is also the best means of putting the information to use. Let employees see the big picture. Give them the balance sheet and teach them to read it.

The intelligence officer in our fighter squadron, Joe Cohn, had a deep concern for people. He saw that while the pilots and crew chiefs were always in on the action, most of the squadron didn't know what was going on. If they could see the bigger picture, he said, they would better understand the importance of their own contribution. It was a great idea. The briefings he set

up brought a tightly knit squadron even closer together and boosted an already high comradeship.

You can find many ways to get the word out, through meetings, telecon-
ferencing, newsletters. One high-performing company puts important staff
meetings on a speaker phone to its regional offices. The important thing is to
hold sharing information as a value of the organization.

• *Praise Openly and Often*

An employee who receives a sincere compliment, especially in front of
other people, is going to be encouraged to do even better. One of the points
of Ken Blanchard's *One Minute Manager* is to give "One Minute Praisings,"
letting people know "in no uncertain terms" when they're doing well.[3] Everybody needs reassurance. This is a good rule to remember: *If you have something good to say, say it here and now.*

• *Killing the Spirit*

On the other hand, if a manager does nothing but criticize or gives no
recognition, employees may feel that they can't do anything right. Therefore,
it doesn't matter what they do. Continual criticism, in the workplace as in a
family, is corrosive to the human spirit.

• *Paychecks and Promotions*

A paycheck or earned bonus has a symbolic as well as an economic function. To the individual it's a tangible sign of approval and encouragement. An
earned raise or promotion signals recognition and demonstrates trust. The
prolonged absence of either sends a different signal. Timing is important.

It's important to work hard on evaluating people for a performance pay
raise. Take the time to write an uplifting but candid and intellectually honest
review from which the person can learn. Create team bonuses for achieving
departmental goals, so that every employee in the company has incentive
compensation, not just sales people. Bonuses also can be an incentive for
specific team goals such as completing training programs. Include everyone
in profit sharing.

The Whole Person

Ford began to prosper when its CEO and then chairman, Donald Petersen,
focused on the human values that make teams work. His approach was essentially this:

To show deep concern for people — give them a chance to live meaningful lives — and to foster an attitude of trust, cooperation, and respect throughout the organization.[4]

Concern for people extends beyond the workplace. Since personal and professional life are closely entwined, it is in the organization's interest for a leader to provide compassion and caring to a troubled employee. This doesn't mean meddling in someone's life, but it does mean offering guidance and support when needed. If a person's effectiveness drops off, the cause may be some personal issue that needs attention. With trust and confidence, a leader can at least help point a person in the right direction. *Listening*, by itself, may enable the individual to begin sorting out the problem. Along the way, the leader will take a hard look in his or her own mirror. The record shows that problems often reside in the upper echelon.

CHAPTER 2

VALUES AND MISSION

The purpose in a man's mind is like deep water,
but a man of understanding will draw it out.
Proverbs 20:5

"Our Values Stink"

A few years ago, we challenged an agency of the U.S. Government to take a hard look at its values. One of the executives said, in effect, "our values stink." This is how he depicted what the organization actually believed in:

> *Get it done on time.*
> *Don't rock the boat.*
> *We already know that.*
> *Accept non-documented facts.*
> *We know what's best for you.*

We challenged the employees to dig beneath the surface and discover what their true values were. As we brainstormed, inner core values began to emerge. The prevailing atmosphere was "us" against "them," and as we worked together, the employees began to emphasize the importance of a "we" situation, as in "we're all in this together." They faced the "don't rock the boat" pattern and identified change as something positive, as opposed to maintaining the status quo. They acknowledged the importance of fairness and equality and came to see the diversity of peoples' backgrounds and skills as a plus.

Managers realized that, to gain the greatest productivity from employees, each individual had to have a major hand in determining the course of his or her own career. In one instance, the agency concluded that an investment in people, rather than technology, would have a greater payoff.

By surfacing deep inner values and clarifying them in discussion and writing, the agency had taken a first step toward creating an atmosphere of cooperation, sharing, and common purpose.

Preparing for the Unknown Future

Heraclitus said, *"All is flux, nothing stays still."*[1] What was true to a Greek philosopher in the fifth century, B.C., is for us the dominant factor of life. Nothing is more certain, more relentless, and more eternal than *change*. Change can be disconcerting, even frightening. We can't always be prepared for it because it often comes to us with little or no precedent. Not being able to see the unknown, we cannot sharpen the right sword, hone the correct skill, assemble the perfect team to meet it. In that great British phrase, sometimes "We just muddle through."

In the early months of 1944, I was a twenty-three-year-old major in the Army Air Forces and had just been assigned to command a squadron of P-47 Thunderbolt fighter-bombers. I loved flying and I was a good flyer, but nothing in my experience prepared me to command three hundred men and lead a squadron of sixteen airplanes into battle.

And no one could fully prepare a pilot for diving into flak, tracer bullets, and cannon fire, when it seemed that the entire German army was bent on killing him. Nor were Iowa farm boys prepared for dealing with the intricacies of superchargers and intercoolers on a 2,000 h.p. engine. But they did it.

For me it was fast, vivid, on-the-job training. With the help of everyone on the team, I learned some basic principles that make an organization work, no matter what the challenge. These principles, refined over the years, remain as valid today as they were then because they are grounded in eternal truths of human nature.

I learned that the best way to prepare for the future, whatever it may bring, is to lay down a solid foundation. Because the unknown and the unprecedented come upon you so quickly, your knowledge alone cannot prepare you for all of the challenges you will meet. You have to have a solid inner guidance system that takes over when you can't see where you're going. That's where *values* come in.

So to deal with the unknown, get in touch with the deep, inner core values that will provide your direction. Things change. Times change. Values do not change.

It Begins with Beliefs

Our fighter squadron was a closely knit team, united in a shared vision and mission. We made it through weather other squadrons could not penetrate to save one of Patton's forward tank units because we had a fighting spirit — an *esprit de corps* that came from an inner core of shared beliefs and values.

The concept of a highly attuned team is an ideal that can be realized by any organization, large or small, but seldom is. Every fighter squadron wasn't first rate, and the vast majority of today's organizations come nowhere near tapping the real wealth of their human resources. To do that may take the most difficult step of all — changing a way of *seeing*. It all begins with the way we believe.

What I learned from the very beginning is that *leadership and management are essentially a matter of basic values.*

Inside each of us is a core of beliefs that acts like a gyrocompass in an airplane. Even though we deviate from our course and at times may be just plain lost, we are still proceeding in some general direction.

The word "belief" comes from the Old English "by-lief," according to Clarence Jordan, founder of the community from which Habitat for Humanity began in rural Georgia. "Lief" is the Old English word for life, so "by-lief" means *the way you conduct your life, or the way you show what you believe.* Your convictions are borne out by your life.

Beliefs are what you hold to be true in your mind, translated into how you act and how you behave. A value is a "what," as in "what do you value?", "what do you put a price on?", "what are you willing to put energy into?" Values are what make us run.

Values

THE SEARCH FOR MEANING

Values are the guiding force of an individual and a society, the moral reference point that defines what is good and what is bad, what is noble and what is base. Values are expressed in actions. With or without our knowing it, they shape our thoughts and behavior. They define who we are.

Values are the focus of man's search for meaning in life. For Aristotle, who said "All things desire God," the goal of human life was happiness and well-being.[2] Spinoza and Kant found an ultimate ideal in human freedom. In Christianity, the highest ideal is love, and the major religions of the world share a conviction that selfishness is the cause of much human misery.

Strictly speaking, "value" is a philosophical concept under the branch of ethics, but for our purposes it is an operating principle, accepted as valid, which can be expressed in any practical form. Values can be as broadly de-fined as beliefs, things, conditions, or business practices for which people and customers have high regard.

THE BASIS FOR DECISION MAKING

As a working definition, values are deeply ingrained principles and beliefs that form the basis for action, both personal and professional.

From the leadership standpoint, values provide the framework for a long-term outlook and are, therefore, the source of *vision*. Because values also de-fine purpose, they are the foundation of the *mission*. Values, vision, and mis-sion are inseparable.

What we believe is expressed in all that we create. An organization that clearly recognizes the worth of the individual gains strength from the dedica-tion of its valued employees. A strong ethical core will build trust within the organization and in its dealings with others. Accepting true service as an ideal provides a long-term purpose that transcends momentary advantage.

Apple co-founder A.C. (Mike) Markkula once said, "The most impor-tant asset we have is a good set of values. We believe 'management by values' is the only way to go." If you want to build a new organization or revitalize an existing one, you have to work from the inside out. True change begins in the heart. It starts with inner core values. Attempting to apply TQM or any other management technique will have little effect if the values and sense of pur-pose are weak.

The most sophisticated management techniques, applied to an organization that is without sound identity and direction, will not fundamentally change anything.

On the other hand, if the core of the organization is sound, the direction is clear to everyone involved, and they are actively committed to following it, any number of solutions will work.

As Walt Disney's brother and business partner, Roy, said, "Decision making is easy when values are clear."

If an organization's values are determined and agreed upon, you won't need extensive policy manuals that dictate what to do in every situation. When the values are clear, the policies are clear to everyone.

VALUE-BASED MANAGEMENT — BEING "BRILLIANT IN THE BASICS"

Marty Berger is vice president of sales for Strategic Technologies, Inc., a highly successful computer technology company in Cary, North Carolina. He has said that the philosophy of caring about people permeates everything the organization does, from hiring new employees to dealing with potential customers. *"It is making a match internally, to build the team, and it is making a shared-values match externally, in deciding who we do business with."*

Value-based management is not rocket science, Berger says. It's being "Brilliant in the basics," which is a quote from Coach Vince Lombardi. Lombardi said that to get to the Super Bowl you had to be "brilliant in the basics:" running, blocking, and tackling.

It's a matter of "breaking it down to the ridiculous," Berger says, which means "supporting, encouraging, training. Keep it simple. Keep in mind the value of people. God didn't create junk. There's value in everybody somewhere."

The Layers of an Onion

Having witnessed both sound and unsound values, value alignment, and nonalignment for more than fifty years, I have concluded this: *values are the foundation of success or failure within an organization.*

I believe that we have both internal and external values that are layered like an onion. The outer layers reflect our conscious, finite, and empirical self, while the inner core represents our infinite, true self.

The value base we frequently see is the outside of the onion. This varies considerably, depending upon a variety of factors such as history, geography, family, culture, and experience. These outer layers are driven by an inflated ego. This is the area of self-centeredness and greed; its pattern is one of domination, control, and judgmentalism.

As you begin to peel back the layers of the onion, you get into more profound levels until you reach the deep, taproot values that I believe are common to the great majority of people. In my opinion, these core values are those of the great religious faiths, as expressed in the Ten Commandments and the Golden Rule, which are present in some form in every major religion. They are universal principles having to do with integrity, charity, justice, and respect for our fellow man. They are selfless rather than selfish, unifying rather than dividing.

The problem is to penetrate the outer surface to get at the core. Stumbling blocks to this process are the drive for power, wealth, and fame; the "What's in it for me?" attitude; and the conviction that "For me to win, you've got to lose." Consistently acting out these external values inflates the ego and thickens the insulation between the two selves.

As some people mature — but not all — the hardened barriers slowly begin to dissolve. In a phrase used by MIT professor Huston Smith, who wrote *The Religions of Man*, it is as if the radiance of God "melts the soul's thick cap."[3]

Once the layers have been penetrated and the core values surfaced, these values have to be integrated with external actions. I believe that some people have reached this level, but very few.

Love

The highest of values embodies the lofty concepts of caring for others, honoring individuals, putting the self aside for a greater cause. All of these nobler impulses have to do with a greater good. To me, the truest expression of these values can be summed up in the word, "love." This term embraces compassion, empathy, caring, reverence, and respect for others. At its basis is acceptance of *responsibility* for ourselves and for our world. Love is the highest ideal we know and the surest path we have toward transcending ourselves.

As the core of a value system, this caring is a strong, positive energy, one that creates harmony rather than dissonance. It does not mean sentimentality, do-gooderism, an absence of critical standards, or allowing anyone — including yourself — to be run over. It implies a balance between the head and the heart. You have to be tough when it's time to be tough. But a true leader also will know compassion.

Huston Smith characterizes Buddha as "one of the great personalities of all time," a blend of the cold and rational balanced with "a Franciscan tenderness." He quotes J.B. Pratt, who said the most striking thing about Buddha was "his combination of a cool head and warm heart, a blend which shielded him from sentimentality on the one hand and indifference on the other."[4]

External values of greed and blind self-interest can propel people to ever higher positions as they step on others. But realizing rewards at the expense of someone else creates a vicious circle. What goes around comes right back to bite you. When the CEO of a corporation makes millions in salary, bonuses, and stock options while employees are being fired or taking a pay cut, the system has gotten out of whack. Similarly, the skinheads of this world will defend the "superiority" of their race or religion with hate and violence, but if they would peel back the layers of the onion, they would discover that *we're all in this together*.

Defining Organizational Values: The Wisdom of Confucius

In a corporation, the definition of values should center on issues that are critical to the organization's purpose and identity. This is not just a matter of ethical behavior. Values should reflect an attitude of respect for every human being, internal and external to the organization, building on people's strengths and respecting their weaknesses and limitations. This is the foundation of a winning spirit. In my opinion, the human being is the supreme value of the organization. Defining values is the first step in the integrated process of developing the *mission statement* and setting *goals and objectives*.

Defining values is a process that begins with the leadership team and then proceeds through successive levels until it has encompassed virtually every member of the organization.

How do you go about surfacing core values?

Here's a method we often use.

After setting the stage with a Big Picture view of people, values, and relationships (alignment) as the inner core of an organization, we hold free-wheeling sessions to stimulate right-brain thinking. We challenge every team member to come up with his or her own definition of how the organization should believe, think, and act. We ask people to consider the corporate viewpoint with regard to people: the organizational team, customers, suppliers, even competitors.

One method we use as a starting point is to draw on the teachings of Confucius, whom the Chinese revere as the First Teacher. In an ancient formula, Confucius expressed the wisdom of aligning values:

If there be righteousness in the heart,
  there will be beauty in the character.

If there be beauty in the character,
  there will be harmony in the home.

If there be harmony in the home,
  there will be order in the nation.

If there be order in the nation,
  there will be peace in the world.[5]

We bring this formula directly into our present organizational world by substituting concepts such as "department" for "home" and "strength in a corporation's business position" for "order in the nation." The concept is to get at the core values, which begin with the individual, permeate the organization, and shape its dealings with the world.

Notice that in the Confucian formula it all starts with righteousness in the heart. Think of this in view of all the people you deal with. What does "righteousness in the heart" mean when you are working with people inside and outside the organization?

We encourage the team members to do some heavy thinking about what is truly important for the organization. We try to draw people out on concepts such as *sincerity, integrity,* and *reliability.* There is no right or wrong. You just write down whatever comes to mind. It takes time and effort, but a consensus eventually emerges.

The purpose is to produce a Statement of Values that everyone agrees on and that you can use as a reference in decision making, planning, and operations. The values statement is what you are all about.

Expressing what is important to the organization doesn't have to be ponderous. Anything goes, as long as your "value" defines *what* and *how* and *who* you want to be. This is a pragmatic exercise. Roll up your sleeves.

One of the most dynamic value statements we have encountered was produced by ZIPCOM, a young, growing high-tech company that integrates telecommunications networks in the southeastern United States. In addition to setting quality and profitability standards, the values defined the kind of atmosphere, people, and relationships the company desired as its corporate culture. These points stand out:

> *Attract exciting people — more than a few of whom are a little offbeat.*

> *Have a supportive, zany, laughter-filled environment where folks support one another and "politics" are as absent as they can be in a human enterprise.*

> *Work with exciting customers who turn us on, who stretch us, customers from whom we can learn and enjoy being around.*

> *Question the way things are done and never, ever, rest on our laurels.*

To make values count, you have to live by them. ZIPCOM's ability to practice what it preaches has paid off in rapid growth, a reputation for quality service, and a robust bottom line.

VALUES ARE LIVING THINGS

Values are not static. They remain meaningful for the organization only if they remain meaningful to the people they affect. John Gardner, former Secretary of Health, Education and Welfare who has written extensively about the need for institutions to renew themselves, says that "values decay over time." A system's values and goals need continual regeneration and reinterpretation — "a perpetual rebuilding."[6]

The corporate Statement of Values is either a living, breathing concept that provides guidance in all phases of operations, from recruiting to decision making, or it's blah blah. It has to be kept current.

Further, value statements won't have much effect if people don't believe the company means what it says. Writing in *Fortune Adviser 1997*, Thomas A. Stewart divided values into "hard" values such as profitability and "soft" values such as integrity and respect for the individual.[7] He found that at one Fortune 500 company, only 45 percent of the employees believed the company lived its "soft" values, and only one in four thought it was sincere in respecting individuals.

Stewart also found that people only buy into the values that match their own and interpret the value statement according to their own beliefs. Over time, he says, "self-interest distorts corporate values," which "gradually evolve away from what the company wants."

> *"Values are living things,"* Stewart writes. *"You can't just stick them in a vase and leave them. You have to manage them. Work with them. Keep them alive."*

Vision

It is written in Hebrews, 11:1, *"Faith is the substance of things hoped for, the evidence of things not seen."*

Vision is the ability to see future states of operation before they exist. But it's not just to see possibilities. *Active vision* is something you make happen. Vision impels action. Norman Vincent Peale said, "Expect a miracle. Make miracles happen."

To me, vision is *a mission you can see in your mind's eye,* even *feel and taste,* one that *encourages commitment.* It is a picture of the future, so real that you can see it happening. The more clearly you can hold this image of where you're going, the more committed you will be to accomplishing the mission. Vision allows you to own the mission.

Mike Vance, the former dean of Disney University, has said, "Vision is the crucial component in the formula for success. It holds the keys to the future."[8]

Ownership of the mission by everyone requires that each level of the organization develop its own statement of mission and goals. To the extent possible, *every member of the team* should have a hand in defining the mission and then revising and updating it.

Vision takes into consideration what is and anticipates what is yet to be. It evolves, for example, from seeing both the needs of customers and clients and the opportunities for meeting those needs. It comes from looking into possibilities, while at the same time seeing what you have and what you can contribute.

Ask yourself, "Where am I right now?" and if you make no changes, where you will be two to five years out. If you don't like what you see, ask "Where would I like to be?" and "Where should we be?" and then figure out how you're going to get there. Start thinking about what this would suggest in terms of setting goals

Without vision, a person, organization, or institution stumbles along, *reacting* to the future. Whatever happens, you do your best to survive. With a vision, you become *proactive* and create your own future.

At the Air Force Instrument Instructor Pilots' School, we taught that if you had to fly into a thunderstorm, your best bet was to relax, maintain your flight *attitude* and general heading, and let your bird toss up and down. If you tried to fight every gust or draft, your reactions could knock you higher and plunge you lower, and you could very well tear up an airplane.

As with in-air refueling, you had to keep your cool. From a distance the basket coming back from the tanker looks stable, but the closer you get to it, the more you can see that it's whipping up and down. If you try to bob around with the basket, you'll never hit it. You have to take a long range view, focus beyond it, and fly a steady course into it.

The point is this: *don't sweat the small stuff.* Vision provides the long-term focus on the mission that stabilizes your operations. As you pursue your goal, it keeps you focused on the big picture and not on every tiny element.

In her book, *Leadership and the New Science*, Margaret J. Wheatley compares vision with a force field in physics, a flow of energy that penetrates every corner of an organization. Vision is similar to unseen but powerful forces such as electromagnetic fields and gravity. "What if we saw a *field of vision*," she asks, "that needed to permeate organizational space, rather than viewing vision as a linear destination?"[9] In her view, vision is like a dynamic force field.

Your vision, written down in inspiring terms, becomes your Mission Statement.

Mission

A MISSION IS ABOUT MEANING

There is still a feeling in corporate America that values and mission statements are fine, but they're icing on the cake and not the cake itself. Corporations are looking for profitability and may believe that it comes from technology or some systematic approach to production. They think people have to fit into a system, rather than the system fitting into people, but that doesn't work. It's a two-way street. The two elements have to fit together. Without sharing in responsibility for defining the organization's mission, employees have no ownership of its purpose.

Viktor Frankl, the Viennese psychiatrist who was imprisoned in a Nazi concentration camp, observed that among his fellow prisoners, the person who lost the will to live "had lost faith in the future." He determined that the one human freedom that cannot be taken away is the freedom "to choose one's *attitude* in any given set of circumstances, to choose one's own way."

"It is this spiritual freedom," he wrote, "that makes life meaningful and purposeful."[10] To survive a person had to make a conscious decision that his own life had meaning.

A *mission* is all about meaning. When you're in an area that has a deep-seated core value to you and you have a commitment to its fulfillment, you're going to succeed. You're going to make it happen.

ABSOLUTE BELIEF IN ACCOMPLISHING THE MISSION

In the summer of 1944, we were flying near the Seine River, trying to stop the German Army from crossing over and regrouping on the other side. Approaching the river, we ran into heavy flak, ugly black puffs of smoke so thick it looked as if you could walk on it. We were dodging and changing altitude, trying to outguess the gunners, when we saw five barges on the water, 10,000 feet below. They were heavily loaded with enemy equipment and troops.

As I rolled into my dive-bomb run, almost straight down, my P-47 Thunderbolt shuddered as heavy shrapnel slammed into the propeller and engine. Oil streamed back to cover my windscreen and the engine rpms screamed up to 50 percent above redline, something that not even the P-47 was built to withstand. If I stayed in the dive, would I ever come out of it?

"You have no option," I said to myself. "You've got to do it!" I had the target perfectly lined up and couldn't quit now. At that moment it was my total focus in life. Punching off my bombs at the last minute, I got direct hits with both. Bobbing and jigging from side to side, and with oil still blowing back, I pulled up and away from the river and the flak. Miraculously, the engine was still running. It carried me to an emergency landing strip in Normandy.

What kept me going was my absolute belief in the mission.

Flying a combat mission in World War II was the end point in a bigger

mission that was embodied in the hopes and aspirations of the American people, from the cities along the East Coast, the farms in the Midwest, the great prairies and mountain ranges, to the shoreline of California. The Big Picture mission was to preserve a society and a way of life which we held dear. To do that, we had to wage war and win. There could be no compromise.

THE MISSION STATEMENT

The mission is derived from values as well as vision.

A *mission statement* is an agreement, committed to writing, as to why an organization exists. The statement should be challenging and attainable. People respond to challenge. It should be exciting, so that people can own it, be inspired by it, and feel pride in carrying it out.

A mission statement is not a slogan. It should answer the questions, "*Who is the customer we serve?*" and "*How well will we provide support?*" Whether the customer is someone in the marketplace or in the organization, the statement should give a clear sense of service and how to make it happen.

Nor is a mission statement a linear destination. Unlike goals and objectives, which have specific endpoints, mission statements project vision and are ongoing. They are like a wellspring. The mission statement establishes a framework of reference and reflects a flow of energy to every part of the organization. As in Margaret Wheatley's analogy, it embodies a "field of vision" that permeates organizational space.

In my view, it was a vision field, an energy of dedication and sense of mission that flowed through our fighter squadron in World War II, giving it an indomitable spirit. I have no doubt that Grumman Aerospace was similarly inspired during the Apollo program. As soon as Grumman defined its mission as not to build rocket hardware, but to put a man on the moon, Charles Garfield, an expert on motivation, says, that statement increased the company's productivity more than 40 percent.[11] Behind Apple Computer's dazzling early success was the founders' commitment to a bold and lofty vision: "To change the world by empowering individuals through personal computing technology."

ZIPCOM, the network integration company, followed up its definition of values with this Statement of Mission:

> *ZIPCOM's mission is to become the largest*
> *customer-oriented network integrator in the Southeast.*
> *This mission will be accomplished by providing highly functional,*
> *comprehensive solutions and world-class service to customers.*
> *ZIPCOM's core values — which include quality service, innovative*
> *work, constant improvement, world-class employees, and*
> *unquestionable honesty — serve as the company's enduring*
> *tenets and guiding principles.*

Each department of the company has its own mission statement. This is the mission of the Engineering Department:

> *To implement solutions that exceed our customers' expectations*
> *while providing the highest level of trust and reliability.*

Engineering is committed to establishing and maintaining long-term symbolic relationships based upon open communication and understanding.

In both statements, the mission is expressed in terms of values as well as purpose, and in both cases, it is ongoing, like a bridge into the future.

Once mission statements are clearly defined, goals, objectives, and action steps follow. These are designed to carry out the mission in a time-phased and measurable fashion.

If you already have a mission statement, don't just say it's done. Go over it, question it, see if it needs refining. Along with reassessing values, mission statements should be thoroughly examined *once a year*, and action plans considered even more frequently.

Successful organizations we work with put considerable time and effort each year into identifying and arriving at solutions to problems/opportunities. This concludes with an annual session attended by all members, concentrating on leadership team building in the morning and then breaking into small solution groups in the afternoon to fine-tune their values, mission, and goals.

We have found that too many mission statements are run-of-the-mill, lack pizzazz, and are void of profound meaning. Maybe they've been created by only a few, who might be out of touch with the people who are making things happen. They could be the product of just trying to get *something* on paper. With such a lackluster effort, it is the rare person who even knows the mission statement exists, let alone is able to recite or explain it. Most importantly, the statement lacks the essential element of support, belief in, and ownership by the workforce at large.

A shared mission, founded on shared values and beliefs, expressed in concrete goals is where *esprit de corps* comes from — the fire within that separates a great organization from an also-ran.

CHAPTER

PLANNING

Failing to plan is planning to fail.
American axiom

Purpose: Seeing the Big Picture

When the Allies landed on D-Day, Rommel said our absolute control of the air "completely paralyzed" the German ability to respond. Under constant aerial bombardment, it took the 2nd Panzer Division seventeen days to move from Toulouse to Normandy, a trip that should have taken three days.[1]

That small but crucial failure was the focal point of a chain of events that, ultimately, flowed from the joint planning staff in Washington. With the D-Day landing, free-roaming Allied planes pounded the enemy whenever and wherever he tried to move. Months before, we had continuously dive-bombed the bridges and railroads the Germans would have to use.

Moving backward from the battlefield, we came under the great umbrella of *strategic planning* for Operation Overlord, which laid out time-phased plans to destroy the Luftwaffe and sweep it from the skies of France. The invasion itself was but part of a grand strategy that would lead to winning the war. Driving that strategy was the Big Picture vision, shared by the Allied nations, of absolute victory.

In any business or other organization, the Big Picture consists of *values, vision,* and *mission.* Together, these elements spell out the organization's definition and purpose — answering the questions, "Who am I?" and "What do

I do?" The Big Picture provides the basis of *strategic planning*, which sets the long-term direction, and for *tactical planning*, which defines short-term goals and objectives.

Success in our world today depends upon everyone owning the mission. To own the mission, each person has to have a hand in developing the group values, vision and mission. By the same token, for planning to really work, it also must be the product of a total group effort. Everybody has to have the opportunity to wrestle with the issues involved, adjust them, make suggestions, and finally, be responsible for the results.

Establishing the Big Picture is no kindergarten exercise. It's the meat and potatoes of organizational development. Everything flows from that.

The Strategy That Built General Motors

In the 1920s, the automobile industry had been dominated for a decade by Henry Ford and his Model T, which was without peer in the low-price, high-volume field. In 1921, Ford sold 60 percent of the cars bought in America. General Motors' market share that year was down to 12 percent.

Alfred Sloan, who headed GM at that time, recounts in his book, *My Years With General Motors*, that GM had no coherent strategy and "no clear cut concept of the business."[2] Not only was General Motors not competitive with Ford on the low end, where the volume and future growth lay, but it was competing against itself in the middle of the market, where it put its main focus.

In 1921, GM developed a strategy to limit the number of models it made and produce a line of cars to cover all price ranges. Knowing that it could not beat Henry Ford at his own game, GM would produce a better car aimed at the top end of Ford's market. While Henry Ford held to his original concept of providing basic transportation, GM realized that the low-end demand could be met by a growing used car market, so it assisted buyers with trade-ins and installment buying. GM's strategy provided what Americans wanted: more luxury and diversity. Henry Ford, for all his genius, could not see that the Big Picture had changed radically.

Plan Backward from a Vision of Success

To achieve success, you first must envision it. Start out with a vision that is lofty and positive. Believe in where you want to go and where you want to be in the future. See yourself there.

If you have doubts about some approach you're going to take, before you make a final decision, ask yourself, "What's the worst thing that could happen?" Then ask yourself, "Okay, if that does occur, can I handle it?" Either you can or you can't. If you can, from that point on, commit yourself and put your whole focus on making it happen.

Aim at a far horizon, establish your assumptions, imagine the future you desire, and then *back into it.* To achieve what you want in year five, ask yourself, what must you do in years four, three, and so on? Direction for the future years will be broad in scope. The closer you get to the present, the more precise and detailed your planning will be.

Ensure that the long-term and short-term goals and objectives are in agreement and are supportive of each other. Planning backward creates an interlocking system that maintains integrity from short-term "actions to be carried out now" all the way back to the definition of core values.

A federal agency we had assisted in creating an eighteen-month strategic plan called us back a year or so later to establish a five-year plan. Having worked with more than 150 people on team building and leadership, we had established a productive relationship of trust and confidence with the agency.

It would have been a simple matter to tweak the plan for FY 94, say, and get FY 95, but then the plan wouldn't have been worth the paper it was written on. We had to look out over the next four to five years and ask, "If we continue doing what we're doing today, will it work?" "What do we need to do to carry out our mission and take care of all the agencies we have to serve?"

The chief administrator and his key people began to think through what they would need five years out and what assumptions we could make. As a consequence, we arrived at a set of guidelines, put them down on paper, and then built a plan around the guidelines. In effect, we backed into it.

Along the way, we recognized that changes *would* occur, and we had to develop a flexible strategy. The goals don't change; you're merely making your course more precise. You're continually looking at it and trying to find a better way, but you're always backing into it. You go backward and forward.

Establishing the Big Picture and planning backward is an ongoing process. You need a fresh assessment every year, an annual review process. Each time, take a hard look at *(1) how you're doing today* and *(2) where you want to be at least five years from now.* Ask yourself, "If we continue to do the same thing we are doing now, where will we be then?" "Is that where we want to be?"

An Approach to Pulling it All Together

Mission Values Vision People Alignment Leadership					
Corporate How can we do better? • Challenges • Opportunities • Ideas • Needs • Prioritize	**Corporate** • Values • Mission • Strategy • Goals	**Departments Teams Projects** How can we do better? • Success factors • Major strength to reinforce • Major weakness to overcome • Programs to discontinue • Prioritize	**Department** • Values • Mission • Goals	**Action Plans** • Specific • Time phase • Measurable • Options • Accountability	**Organizational Actions** **Everyone's Actions** **Individual Actions**

Planning

Strategic — **Tactical** — **Execution**

Know where you want to go and why. Identify how to get there. Back into it.

COMMIT YOURSELF

You can't achieve any goal until you've made up your mind that you're going to do it. Making that decision is the all-important step of commitment. Commitment is the energizing factor. It focuses your determination and your energies toward accomplishing what you have set out to do. Commitment is no halfway, "maybe I will and maybe I won't" matter. It's not ambiguous. True commitment is investment of the heart as well as the mind.

Be positive about it. If your focus is negative, you can't do it. You're wasting your time.

And don't get into second-guessing yourself. At the time you made the decision, you did it based on the best information available to you. If you're wrong, be flexible, but don't get bogged down in questioning everything you've done.

As baseball great Satchel Paige once said, *"Don't look back. Something might be gaining on you."*

Strategy: Finding Focus and Setting Your Goals

LONG-TERM PERSPECTIVE

Harvard sociologist Dr. Edward Banfield set out to discover why some people became financially independent during their lifetime. What was it, he asked, that made them so successful? Why were they different from other people? At the outset, he was convinced that the answer would be found in family background, education, intelligence, influential contacts, and other such developmental factors.[3]

To his surprise, he found that the main reason for success in life was not in the obvious advantages. It was in an attitude, a state of mind. He called this attitude "*long-term perspective.*"

In his 1970 book, *The Unheavenly City,* Banfield published his findings showing *that the most successful men and women in life and the most likely to move up economically were those who considered the future in every decision they made in the present.* He found that the longer the time period a person considered while planning and acting, the more likely it was that he or she would be an outstanding achiever.

STRATEGIC PLANNING

ESSENTIAL & POWERFUL

IF

- **INNOVATION IS ALIVE, WELL & FLOURISHING.**

- **EVERYONE IS IN ON THE ACT.**

- **FLEXIBILITY UNDERSTOOD & ACCEPTED.**

STRATEGIC PLANNING

Strategic planning is a means of setting long-term direction. It translates the values, vision, and mission statement into a definition of *where you want to go* and *what you want to achieve.* The end point is action. Looking ahead to where your organization or team wants to be five to ten years into the future, figure out what course you have to take and what major tasks you have to accomplish to get there. Because no one can predict what will happen five years from now, the strategic plan has to be broad and flexible. Tactical planning will focus on the details.

HOW TO THINK AND ACT STRATEGICALLY
PRINCIPLES VS. "HOW-TO'S"

1. CULTIVATE VISION AT <u>ALL</u> LEVELS… BUT <u>DON'T</u> ESCAPE REALITY.

2. RECOGNIZE EVERYBODY HAS "CUSTOMERS"… AND USE COMPETITIVE ADVANTAGE.

3. FOCUS, FOCUS, FOCUS… AND REFOCUS!

4. MAKE <u>CONTINUOUS</u> MID-COURSE CORRECTIONS.

5. LEVERAGE RESOURCES: STRENGTHS… SUCCESSES… FLEXIBILITY… AND CRITICAL TALENT.

6. MEASURE, MEASURE, MEASURE… AND TAKE ACTION!

7. ELIMINATE "NON-ESSENTIAL"… REDUCE "ESSENTIAL" AND INVEST IN "HIGH RETURN."

8. STRESS <u>BOTH</u> ACHIEVEMENT AND IMPROVEMENT OPPORTUNITIES.

9. BREAK BIG PROBLEMS INTO SMALL, "MANAGEABLE" ACTION.

10. PRESERVE <u>POSITIVE</u> "ORGANIZATIONAL MEMORY"… BUT AVOID "ALWAYS DONE THIS WAY" OR "WE ARE DIFFERENT."

11. BE PREPARED FOR ROAD BLOCKS… ESPECIALLY "SECOND GUESSERS."

12. TURN PROBLEMS INTO OPPORTUNITIES.

STRATEGY VS. PLANNING

STRATEGY	PLANNING
• <u>"Total Picture"</u>	• <u>Departmental</u>
• Anticipate <u>Future</u>	• Project <u>Current</u>
• "What <u>Should</u> Be"	• "What <u>Will</u> Be" and "<u>How</u>"
• Focus on <u>Issues</u>	• Focus on <u>Financial</u>
• <u>Guide</u> and <u>Assess</u> Plans	• Bottom Up <u>Projections</u> (Overly Optimistic)

THE MULBERRY HARBORS

The D-Day landing at Normandy in June 1944 was the greatest amphibious operation in the history of the world. The success of the invasion depended upon deceiving the Germans as to where the landing would come, so the Allies conceived an *elaborate strategy* to convince Hitler that they would land at Calais, rather than at Normandy. Calais was the shortest point across the Channel from England, and its coast had the deep-water ports that would be vital for sustaining any invasion.

To provide the ports that the Normandy landing zone did not have, Churchill determined in 1942 to create artificial ports and tow them across the Channel. It was a bold, incredibly audacious concept. The system consisted of sinking ships as a breakwater and towing huge concrete caissons through high seas, to be sunk near the French coast and connected to the shore with floating quays and ramps.

Although the two Mulberry Harbors were soon damaged in heavy storms and one was destroyed, they made the invasion in Normandy possible, allowing for it to be supported and reinforced in its most crucial hours. They also played a critical role in the deception plan. Hitler knew that no army could sustain an invasion without harbors, and he held his tanks in Calais until it was too late.

These are examples of fulfilling the mission statement:
- GM creating its own niche by building on the public need for luxury

and diversity, while satisfying the continuing need for basic transportation through used cars and trade-ins and installment buying.

•   Churchill's reinforcing the German expectation that the invasion of France would take place at the Channel's narrowest point (less than twenty miles), where ample ports were available, while making plans to cross at its widest point (more than 100 miles) by towing in temporary harbors.

ESTABLISH FOCUS: HOW CAN WE DO BETTER?

Strategic direction is set by the leadership team and expressed in a strategy statement. The *Strategy Statement* in theory is a framework that guides choices about the nature and direction of an organization. It explains where you are going and how you will get there.

In writing strategy statements, ask yourself: "Who are our clients or customers?" "How can we uniquely serve their needs?" "How can we build on our strengths and successes?" "How can we 'ride the wave,' innovating, seeing new trends and approaches, taking advantage of new technology?" "How can we maximize the talents of our people?" Start with the phrase, "We will strive to...."

Strategic and tactical planning are an immediate followup to defining core values and mission and are accomplished in the same kind of no-holds-barred brainstorming sessions. Making the process work requires an atmosphere of trust. It has to be clear that no one's going after personalities, only organizational functions. Repeating the process in teams or solution groups is not redundant. Direction has to be understood, and goals have to be refined at every level.

Prior to the annual planning session, the leadership team will have spent a good bit of time in preparation, perhaps identifying the organization's ten major problems. To establish *focus*, leadership will then prioritize the problems and deal with, say, the top four.

The issues are: *How can we do better? How can we improve the way we work together? What new ideas can we put to work?* Look at your strengths and short suits. What are the challenges and opportunities? What activities should you be emphasizing? Which ones are giving returns? If something is not giving a return, should it be dropped?

You can begin with preliminary questionnaires to get ideas flowing, simple flip charts that pose questions, or exercises that stimulate thinking. Focus attention not only on internal concerns such as management productivity and employee attitudes, inventory controls, cost accounting, etc., but also on external issues, such as trends, supplier operations, customer profiles, market niche and, very importantly, the competition.

Dr. Ichak Adizes, author of *The Pursuit of Prime*, says that in diagnosing problems in a company, it is important to distinguish between internal and external integration. External integration is about identifying clients and satisfying the needs of customers, while internal integration has to do with coordinating efforts within the company. "When an organization devotes more effort to internal than to external integration, " he writes, "sales and profits begin to deteriorate, customer service slackens, and repeat orders decline." Under the laws of physics, energy expended internally is not available for external efforts. The company, Adizes says, needs "organizational equilibrium."[4]

STRATEGIC PLANNING EXERCISES

Here are three typical exercises to help you get started on strategic planning. Take a few minutes now to begin thinking through what your *Ideal Organization* would look like and what you should be doing now to build toward it (p.38). Look at your *Success Factors*, from most to least successful, and question why they are that way (p.39). Finally, think about your *Strengths and Weaknesses* and what you should be doing about each (p.40).

You Can't Plan Without Teamwork

We had a contract a few years ago with an agency of the federal government to produce a strategic plan for an information processing division. When we spoke with the key people in order to fine-tune the program to their specific needs, we found that we'd walked into a minefield. The heads of the organizations weren't working together, and the employees were deeply divided on a crucial issue of changing technology.

The division had installed an IBM mainframe system in the 1960s to track a massive document flow. By the time we were called in, it had been in operation for some thirty years. Newer and better software was becoming available, and the division chief charged straight ahead to begin implementing a vastly improved system. He ignored the fact that his entire staff had jobs that were linked to the past.

He created an "Advanced Projects Section," which in effect made everyone else feel, "We're the retards." People were divided between the "Advanced

IDEAL ORGANIZATION

The way you see your organization right now:	If we do nothing differently, where will we be in 1-3-5 years from now?
The way you would like to see your organization:	The way your organization would benefit:

Commitment: What should we be doing <u>now</u>? <u>This year</u>. What's holding you back? What goals does this suggest?

_____

_____

_____

_____

_____

_____

SUCCESS FACTORS

Identify 2 or 3 programs or activities which you consider most successful, and note 2 or 3 which you consider least successful. Then consider the distinctions. What have been the causes or key factors involved in success or lack of success?

Most Successful	Least Successful
1.	1.
2.	2.
3.	3.

Distinctions and Causes

Successful when or because…	Less successful when or because…

STRENGTHS AND WEAKNESSES

Major Strengths	To Reinforce Strengths

Major Weaknesses	To Overcome Weaknesses

Projects" people and the "Dinosaurs." There were signs on the wall, "We're Dinosaurs and Proud of It!" To make the situation worse, a lot of the staff didn't want to change anything. Their attitude was, "Don't bother me. I'm not going to learn anything new. I'll be gone from here in three years." Several section heads who had been at their jobs for twenty years were fighting our attempts to have them fill out personal assessments such as the Myers-Briggs preference inventory. "Why do we have to be tested?" they asked. "We're doing all right the way things are."

It became clear to us that we had to conduct a team building session if we expected to carry out a successful strategic planning program. The federal government being what it is, this would have taken a contract redo and a six-month delay, so we swallowed the cost ourselves. It worked. Once it became clear that we were sincerely interested in improving operations, rather than merely conducting an exercise for the record, things began to fall into place. By the end of a three-day planning session, the group had produced a creative set of strategic plans. We received a 9.1 out of a possible 10 rating and went on to facilitate the development of a five-year strategic plan for four echelons of management.

The lesson we learned was that *you can't do effective strategic planning unless you have a basis of understanding and cooperation.* Team building had to come first.

Thomas Edison, who is too often thought of as a loner, credited much of his success to teamwork. Rather than working in isolation, he was always involved with others. He said, "You never saw such a mixed crew as we had at Menlo Park. We all worked as a team."[5]

Establish Meaningful Goals

The articulation of a goal should be more than a cut-and-dried, numerical statement of fact. Like the mission statement, it should create meaning for employees and become a source of inspiration. It should play to people's hearts as well as to their minds. John Kennedy's declaration that the United States would land a man on the moon within the decade was an awesome challenge that stirred a sense of pride in the hearts of Americans. It was we who were going to the moon, not they of NASA. Inspiring goals can unite people.

In their book, *Competing for the Future*, Gary Hamel and C.K. Prahalad say that a goal should command the allegiance and respect of every employee.[6]

Goals should carry a sense of destiny and should be focused on making a real difference in the lives of customers.

They tell about talking to employees at an electronics plant who had been constantly urged to do better, try harder, improve quality and costs, but were never told *why*. They couldn't name their major global competitor or tell why they were more or less competitive than the rival, and they had no idea of the productivity issues such as market share, growth, and innovation. They couldn't get interested in the game because they had no meaningful scorecard.

The "strategic intent" of the company should be imparted in goals which appeal to the emotion as well as to the intellect, Hamel and Prahalad say. In return for employee loyalty and diligence, senior management has the responsibility to imbue their work with "a higher purpose than a paycheck." *The company should have an emotionally compelling and broadly shared intent.*

A goal simply to reach a certain size is unlikely to capture the imagination of employees, Hamel and Prahalad say. "While the quest for growth is intrinsic to almost any strategic intent, the real emotional *umph* comes when a company can articulate what it is growing toward." *Only extraordinary goals provoke extraordinary efforts.*

To determine your goals, take a total look at the strategy — what your organization wants to do and can do. Make the goals focus on the mission statement. Look at the Big Picture and ensure that individual actions are a productive part of the whole. Think of what you want to achieve one, two, three, or five years out. Take a "total look."

Develop options, set priorities, and establish a means for measuring success. Take action and keep yourself up-to-date through regular feedback and measurement.

Indicate the *why* of every goal. Spell out what you intend to accomplish so that what people do makes sense to them and earns their commitment.

Tactics/Action Plans

Tactical Planning is short-term planning of actions to make goals happen. The Action Plan normally would *include the results you expect, specific steps, responsibility and accountability, the measurement of success, options, target dates for starting and ending, and dates for review.*

At a minimum, the plan should: *(1) cover the tasks necessary to carry out each goal or objective,* and *(2) identify the responsible individual or teams and the completion date.*

Following is a simple Action Plan format with a typical example that helps an organization get at values, mission, goals and tactics in the shortest possible time. We have used these tools successfully for more than 10 years.

TACTICAL PLANNING

Actions To Make Goals Happen

- **Specific**
- **Time–Phased**
- **Measurable**
- **Options**
- **Accountability**

Options and Contingency Planning

In *The Bridge on the River Kwai*, a British intelligence officer says prophetically before setting off on a mission, *"There's always the unexpected. Isn't there?"*

Sometimes conditions are such that no matter how much skill, energy, and willpower you put into a project, you'll find you cannot reach the target as planned. You always need an option, a contingency plan to fall back on.

In countless situations during a career of flying, getting back on the ground with myself and my plane in one piece depended upon anticipating trouble and knowing what to do before it happened.

In flying, the pilot has to have an alternate destination in case the weather at the primary destination is below VFR (Visual Flight Rules) minimums and make detailed preparations for landing there, with the necessary maps and let-down plates. Once when I was flying into Panama City, Florida in a new, all-weather jet fighter, I ran into a heavy thunderstorm. The sky grew dark. Lightning flashed, green St. Elmo's fire flickered across the windscreen, and

SHORT FORM ACTION PLAN

Department: _____

Values; Mission; Goals; Action

Values	
Mission	
Goals	Long Term 5 Years Short Term 1 Year

Action

	Description	Assign To	Complete Date
1			
2			
3			
4			
5			

DEPT: *Engineering*
Mission, Goals, Tactics
Fiscal Year 1998

Vision:	To grow the engineering group to become Nationally Recognized as the leading Infrastructure Architects.
Values:	The engineering team strives to be a major contributor to the success of Strategic Technologies. We strongly believe in a commitment to our customers which includes honesty and integrity where we do what we say an "say only what we can do." We also believe in the camaraderie of our team and the desire for individual growth.
Mission:	To design and implement infrastructure solutions and provide a support mechanism for all of STI's solutions. To maintain and enhance our reputation for legendary customer service through responsiveness, efficiency and expertise. To continually support the professional and personal growth of engineers and foster a healthy working environment.
Goals:	• Increase Profitability of Engineering Organization • Improve Engineering Business Processes • Maintain High Employee Retention • Offer New Products and Services • Ensure Proper Knowledge Growth

Tactics:

	Description	Assign To	Complete Date
1	Ensure we are Getting Paid for the Professional Services we are Providing More Effective Utilization of Resources Increase Sales Awareness of Why our Services Should be Paid For Develop Incentives for Increasing Professional Services	MW, GF	1/98
2	Achieve Revenue in Sun Implementation of $18M with Margin of 16.5% Achieve Revenue in HP Implementation of $5.5M with Margin of 15% Achieve Revenue in NT Implementation of $1.7M with Margin of 42% Achieve Revenue in Support of $3M with Margin of 27% (Not including RSM)	MW GF RF MSt	9/98
3	Assign STORM calls to OE to track accurate profitability of individual maintenance contracts	PM, CB	1/98
4	Develop, Document, and Implement a Pre-sales Support Mechanism	SW, JF, MSt	9/98
5	Create Virtuality Among Engineers in All Offices	CF, RF	5/98
6	Employ a More Effective Project Management Process	BW	3/98
7	Develop Long Term Application Support Strategy	MSt, BCl	6/98
8	Purchase and Implement Required Infrastructure and Tools	JC, PW, JL	2/98
9	Cross-Department Internal Process Training Program for New Hires	BCh, HM, JW	4/98
10	Keep STI Employees Who are at Customer Sites in Touch with Internal STI Activities	MSh, TP, CF	6/98
11	Set Realistic Travel Expectations During Interview Process	DS, MSa	2/98
12	Develop Growth Paths	SW	5/98
13	Continue Execution of Retention Plan and Reevaluate	BCl	3/98
14	Review Incentive Compensation	DH	6/98
15	Productize Disaster Recovery	RM	9/98
16	Productize Remote Systems Monitoring	MSt, JC	7/98
17	Develop, Document, and Implement Dept-Wide Training Plan	SW, ER	11/97
18	Implement Training Lab for Our Internal Use	PW, ST	1/98
19	Publish Articles	MSp, DS	9/98

hail was banging on the metal skin of the aircraft. With a sudden jolt, the radios and most of my navigational instruments went out. There was no way I could reach my objective, so with my magnetic compass I set a course for Tampa, my alternate.

Unable to communicate with the tower, I flew over the field, waggling my wings in the emergency signal, and was flashed a green light to come on in. As I rolled to a stop, a crowd of staring people was gathering. When I climbed down, I saw why. The black radar nose of the airplane had been sheared off, and chunks of ice were packed in what had been the nose section. Broken wires and cables dangled from the hole. I did some staring myself.

You have to have a plan for bad weather even if, when you take off, the weather is clear. The same holds true for pursuing any major goal, personal or professional. You might be aiming for X number of new accounts, or the purchase of new equipment, or the launching of a new project. Put real energy, however, into blocking out your options. If things become hopelessly compromised, you have a Plan B or Plan C to fall back on. If you can live with the alternative, you never have to back down to an unacceptable position.

Falling back on an alternative, however, does not mean that you have to give up on your original goal. If the goal is of major importance, learn from the experience and go after it another time — in a different way, if need be.

Opting for Plan B often has unexpected and beneficial returns. In any situation where the unexpected happens, before you give in to painting the whole picture gray, look for the positive side. It's rare to find that any situation is *all* bad.

After leaving the Air Force, I entered the career development field. I was offered a contract by a firm that provided ample dollars per month, so I went out and bought a house for my wife and our two younger sons. The dollars we had agreed to in a contract, however, did not materialize. As Robert Louis Stevenson once put it, I found myself suffering a "financial fluctuation." With a family to support, I suddenly was on the brink of losing our home, along with much more.

I had to react fast, so I developed a three-point contingency plan:

    (1) Hold off my creditors for three months.

    (2) Earn immediate cash through some other employment track.

    (3) Find a new job, using my most marketable skills.

The plan worked. The creditors obliged, and I found a temporary job that was honest and served my purpose. Then I had the good fortune to go to work for Dr. W.J. Reckmeyer, a "systems" genius.

The contingency plan saved our home. It also provided me with new skills in systems engineering. I saw how working with the whole rather than simply with its component parts led to greater efficiency and higher performance. The systems approach led to my career focus on helping people fulfill their lives in all areas — not just on the job. This mission, which has been tremendously rewarding for my wife Marilyn and for me, is something I might not have ever discovered had it not been for my falling back on Plan B.

Here's a personal insight that has become increasingly clear to me over the years:

> *Positive and profound returns of greater and lesser consequence seem to occur to me with increasing frequency. As I become more and more aware of these occurrences and think back on each, I frequently feel a providential hand in the act.*

Backups Are Like Options — You Always Need Them

Over-account for challenges. That way, you won't come up short. When it was critical for our fighter squadron to launch four airplanes on a short alert, we'd have *five* ready to go. One was our backup. Flying out of England, if we needed sixteen aircraft over a target, we would send eighteen. Once the primary sixteen birds were in the air and well over the Channel with all systems "go," the two backups could break off and return to base.

Murphy's Law, like the devil, lurks in the details. Often, it's the small things that will get you, as anyone who has ever arranged a conference knows. In managing a team, make sure people are cross-trained to cover all bases. Expend the time, effort, and resources to have someone capable of filling every essential role.

And just as there are backup brake systems on your automobile, it's smart to provide for a backup bulb for a film or slide projector, an extra roll of film and spare batteries for that special family outing, flashlights and candles for when thunderstorms shut down the power.

You can hope for miracles, but it's best not to expect them.

The Unseen Hand of Providence

Occasionally, when Marilyn and I get into a predicament in scheduling, we find ourselves stymied as to how to resolve the problem. Suddenly, out of the blue, an unseen hand puts everything in order. Once, for example, we inadvertently scheduled ourselves to put on two workshops for different groups on the same day. The first had been set for many months, but somehow it had not been transferred to our new calendar. As we were trying to figure out how to get out of the mess diplomatically, the project officer telephoned from one of the firms and apologetically asked if we might reschedule, due to a problem on his side.

We may be inconvenienced by some major delay and then find that the time we lost was just what we needed to bring a task to a better outcome. In writing, an insight that has never before occurred to us may come suddenly from nowhere. Sometimes the unexpected works out better than anything we had planned — as if it were exactly what was meant to be.

To my mind, this is *Providence*.

CHAPTER

CREATIVITY

Whatever you can do, or dream you can...
BEGIN IT
Boldness has genius, power, and magic in it.
Johann Wolfgang von Goethe

Resourcefulness and Intuition

Like a fighter pilot with an Me-109 on his tail, the leader of a company or public institution always has someone shooting at him. The skies over Europe were hazardous during World War II because they were filled with flak, cannon fire, and machine-gun bullets. In corporate America, bullets are ricocheting all over the place, but they're in the form of nuisance lawsuits, shady if not dishonest undertakings, unfair advertising, industrial espionage, employee intrigue, office politics, and any number of other disagreeable occurrences.

Resourcefulness and intuition are essential tools in your survival kit. There will be moments of decision for which no MBA or other management training can prepare you. That's when quick thinking, knowing you can rely only on your gut instinct, becomes crucial.

I once had to do some fast reacting on a fighter mission over France. I was looking for something to strafe, but the German positions seemed to be pretty well camouflaged. Finally, I spotted movement. It was only a single vehicle, but I thought it might lead to some unit hidden in the trees. Starting a shallow dive, I switched on my guns and tightened my finger on the squeeze trigger.

You can't help but notice when a P-47's coming at you, but the vehicle didn't run for cover. Strange, I thought. Something *seemed* wrong, so at the last second I held my fire.

"My God!" I said aloud. "That's an Army jeep!" It had the windshield folded down over the white star on its hood. The GIs riding in it looked up and waved wildly as I swooped past. My blood went cold. Those guys had no idea how close they'd come to buying the farm.

A great organization is a network in which people relate closely and openly with each other. In a creative, innovative atmosphere, instincts are honed to a high degree. Performance may depend upon a leader or a team coming to the right intuitive decision, and often there isn't much time for deliberation. A competitor drops prices drastically, and you have to decide whether to follow suit, hold steady, or even underbid. Or two members of your team are suddenly at odds, and there's no rational explanation for their behavior, nor a logical clue as to how to resolve the impasse. Can you rely on your instincts to guide you through sorting out the problem?

Close relationships are key at such moments. So are basic values. You have to learn to know and trust your own instincts and also have an appreciation for the best instincts of others. It may not be the leader himself or herself who has the best take on the situation. But the leader has to recognize the best solution, wherever it comes from.

Sometimes all you have to go on is a gut feeling. More often than not, intuition is more reliable than intellect.

The Magic of Commitment

There is magic in the power of commitment. Commitment is like a threshold between possibility and creation.

A casual romantic relationship with another person is different from a marriage. True marriage means that two people are determined in their intent to spend their lives together, no matter what. Knowing that they are committed in their hearts to each other makes it much easier to weather the storms of life and to practice, however imperfectly, patience, forgiveness, and love. They have a bond, a deeply vested interest, and a covenant between them that is a great source of strength. In a casual relationship, you can always pack up your socks and move on.

Commitment means taking action. Its nature is boldness and courage.

Commitment moves beyond the illusory world of infinite possibility to the real world of making a choice and taking a chance. Commitment defines reality. Only if we take action and do something will we ever know what we can do and who we are.

With commitment to a task, a job, a role, a career, all sorts of things begin to happen. W.H. Murray has written that before people are committed, there is hesitancy, and since they're hedging their bets by retaining the chance to draw back, they remain ineffective. There is one elementary truth, he says, concerning all acts of initiative and creation. "*The moment one definitely commits oneself, then Providence moves, too.*"

The decision triggers a whole stream of events. Things happen that would not otherwise have occurred, unforeseen incidents and positive events that no one could have dreamed of.

Commitment is the decisive step in making things happen. Creativity follows commitment.

Make the Creative Process Work for You

Do you ever go to sleep on a problem and then wake up in the middle of the night and have the answer? Almost everyone has done this at some time in their lives. The creative sequence has no doubt worked for you countless times before, but you may not have been aware of it. By knowing how it works and being receptive to it, you can greatly increase its effectiveness.

The process was discovered in the 1920s by a British writer, Graham Wallas. Dr. Willis Harman, president of the Institute of Noetic Sciences, has explained that it involves four steps:[1]

- *Preparation*
- *Incubation*
- *Illumination*
- *Validation*

PREPARATION

If you've decided to do something in your personal or professional life, you're already in the preparation stage. You've made a commitment. In this phase, you define the *need*. The greater the need and the greater the effort, the greater will be the return. Go about it casually and you'll get casual results.

INCUBATION

Internalize the issue you are working on to find a path to your deeper self, the core of inspiration that lies within you. Tell yourself you want an answer and let your internal self work for you. Sleep on it, walk, run, swim, whatever. Don't force the issue and don't expect the answer right now. As you learn to trust the process, it will come.

Mozart's inspiration came when he was alone and relaxed, traveling in a carriage after a good meal. Passages of music would emerge and gradually become more defined until all at once he could hear an entire symphony in his mind. Robert Louis Stevenson referred whimsically to "the little people" who did half his work during his sleep, "God bless them."[2]

For the incubation process to work, you have to be relaxed. Step back from your problems and give yourself a break. Let it happen.

ILLUMINATION

This is the insight, the "*aha!*" Whenever the inspiration comes, *write it down*, even on a scrap of paper. It can be so vivid at the moment, and then in an instant, it's gone. Writing the insight down says to your inner self, "Flag this."

VALIDATION

Check it out. Ask yourself, "Does this make sense?" But don't be too quick about dumping ideas that seem far out. They might be the *breakthrough*.

This is where you take action, which is the whole point. Nolan Bushnell, founder of Atari Corporation, said, "Everyone who's ever taken a shower has an idea. It's the person who gets out of the shower, dries off, and does something about it that makes a difference."

It's amazing how many of us keep plodding along, doing the same old stuff. We come to realize it's not working, but instead of finding a new way, we work harder and faster, digging ourselves deeper into a hole.

Remember *The First Rule of Holes: "If you're in one, stop digging."*

Identify the Problem

You can spend a lot of energy and throw a great amount of resources at solving a problem, but your efforts won't be effective unless you've first *identified the problem correctly.*

I walked into a real mess when I was assigned to the 50th Tactical Fighter

Wing in Hahn, Germany. The wing had just failed its Operational Readiness Inspection — a serious matter indeed — and as Director of Operations, my job was to turn it around. The Wing carried a heavy NATO responsibility. It was the only U.S. Air Force unit in Europe with a "dual strike" mission, which meant that it had to train in both nuclear and conventional armament procedures.

Nobody was happy. These guys were highly qualified, and despite their long hours and hard work, they had failed. My first task was to *listen and learn.* Tearing up the pea patch, fixing blame, firing people was just going to make things worse. I talked to people in every part of the operation and found that they were bright, dedicated, and showed initiative and resourcefulness. The *people* weren't the problem.

As it turned out, the difficulty was in the highly complicated nuclear release procedures, which were different for the U.S. and NATO. The 50th's written instructions had become so complex that they were virtually unworkable. We cleared the decks, simplified, tested, evaluated, and trained. As a result, the 50th passed its next ORI with flying colors and went on to become one of the best fighter units in all of Europe. When Secretary of Defense Robert McNamara or the chief of the Air Force, Curtis LeMay, came to Europe and had time to visit only one organization, the 50th was consistently the one selected.

Brainstorming to Find the Best Solution

The purpose of conventional brainstorming is to surface ideas. Pure brainstorming is the first stage of our approach, but we take it a step further — into the realm of arriving at the best solution.

Over time I have come to deeply appreciate the great creative value of brainstorming. I also have learned that no group can brainstorm effectively in a void. Recall the government agency in which we had to do team building to create a positive atmosphere before we could begin brainstorming on their strategic planning. The bedrock condition for creative group dialogue is *trust.*

With a relationship of trust established, you're ready to release individual and group creativity to seek new ideas and solutions. We have found that certain guidelines are helpful in getting the most out of the brainstorming sessions. These can be expressed in nine rules:

1. Everybody should be free to speak and float ideas.
Every idea, in the first round at least, is valid. Nobody should fear being shot down by others in the group. There are no stupid ideas. The only stupid idea is the one you don't bring up.

2. Define the issue to be brainstormed carefully.
Just what is the problem? Describe the issue in as much detail as possible and don't get distracted from it.

3. Mix people in groups across fields of expertise.
You'll be surprised to see how engineers can come up with solutions to sales problems, and believe it or not, sales people can help solve engineering problems.

Throughout the process, from here on it's a no holds barred, wide open approach, laying cards on the table, weighing issues, not personalities, being diplomatically sensitive (sans fisticuffs), but going all out to identify the best solution.

4. Start in a large group, then break into small groups.
Give the small groups responsibility for brainstorming subsets of the overall problem, then have the small groups report on their results to the large group. In this way, everyone gets a chance to see progress that's been made on all fronts.

5. In the second round, eliminate duplicate ideas.
Identify and discard ideas that overlap or, in real terms, amount to the same thing.

6. Ask the group to vote on the ideas that have come up.
Rank the ideas on a scale of 1 to 5, with 5 being very, very important (or critical).

7. Narrow the focus to the top **four or five** *ideas, based on the results of the vote.*

8. Assign the ideas to small groups to continue the brainstorming.
The small groups will continue brainstorming to develop the ideas — as new products, solutions to systems glitches, or whatever.

9. When you arrive at a solution, TAKE ACTION! Carry out whatever plan you come up with.

The worst thing you can do is to stagnate and fail to put into practice the best results of your brainstorming process. This will demoralize everybody and make future brainstorming sessions much less productive, because people will not believe that their creative efforts will ever count for anything. So be pro-active. Make a commitment. Follow through and get the job done.

The Power of Belief

Remember the Power of Belief, as stated by Henry Ford: *If you think you can, or if you think you can't, you're always right.*

Sheer Panic

One of the most profound learning experiences of my life took place when I was commanding a Fighter Group in Korea in the 1950s. I had been ordered to report to the commanding general of Fifth Air Force, and after returning my salute, the general got up, paced the floor, and began to talk about major problems in his command. Pounding his fist on the table, he said, "I'm sick and tired of all these accidents. And there's no standardization in air tactics. We've got one outfit doing things one way and one doing them another."

"Shook," he said, "I want you to fix it."

He said he wanted me to set up a series of one-week training schools for every commander and operations officer in Korea. I had three weeks to get it done.

Three weeks? I was supposed to start a new school, design the curriculum, put together a staff, and find a location for it in three weeks? My first reaction was sheer panic.

I spent that first week researching the problem, and the more I looked at it, the bigger and more impossible the tasks ahead became.

I also did a lot of praying. In my utter frustration I picked up my Bible and by chance opened it to the book of James. My eyes fell upon, *"Consider yourself fortunate when all kinds of trials come your way."*

"I qualify there," I said to myself. "Now what?"

"But if any of you lack wisdom," it continued, *"he should pray to God."*

I'm doing that until I'm blue in the face, I thought. So why can't I move this mountain? I read further and found, *"But you must believe when you pray, and not doubt at all; for whoever doubts is like a wave in the sea that is driven and blown by the wind."*

Then it came to me. *I DIDN'T BELIEVE I COULD DO IT.* All I was focusing on was my own internal dialogue, the negative tapes in my head that were playing the same message over and over. "You haven't got a prayer, Charlie." "You're gonna blow this one."

WITH GOD AS MY COPILOT

Suddenly, the light came on. I knew that with *faith in myself* and with God as my copilot, I could do the job. The only thing that had been holding me back was the belief that I couldn't.

I had a vision of the accident rate going down and tactics being improved so that everybody's working together, going down the same track. With a clear vision of the Big Picture — the need to standardize tactics and procedures so that the Fifth Air Force could operate effectively and save lives — I worked backward to solve individual problems. First, I had to get the right *people* in, people I could rely on. I chose three pilots I trusted and asked them to find more men we could count on. They had to be first-class pilots who could talk and listen and be respected, and who could have *fun*. Everything began to fall into place.

Keeping in mind, "the good Lord's right by my side," I would no sooner think through a problem than I'd have an answer for it. Miraculously, we opened the school on time and graduated twelve one-week courses. The training was so successful that it was extended to all of Japan, in addition to Korea.

There's only so much room in your noggin. If you fill 90 percent of it with negative thoughts, there's little room left for the positive.

THE CHEMISTRY OF BELIEF

A man had been accidentally locked in a railroad refrigerator car. The next morning, he was found huddled in a corner, dead. He had tried to claw the door open in a futile attempt to escape. An autopsy determined that the man had frozen to death, or in medical terminology, had died of hypothermia.

Contrast this with another story, of a five-year-old boy in Texas who suffered from a malignant brain tumor. The prognosis was dismal. Using techniques devised by Dr. Carl Simonton, every day the boy visualized the tumor getting smaller and smaller. One day when he was asked again to visualize the tumor, he could no longer see it. X-rays showed that the tumor was gone.

These stories are told by Dr. Jim Conner, a North Carolina educator who is a friend and a former member of the 506th Fighter Squadron.[3] One is about death and the other is about a new lease on life — each an example of the incredible power of belief.

But what does a man freezing to death have to do with belief? We omitted one all-important fact. *At no time, while the man was in the railroad car, did the temperature go below 60 degrees Fahrenheit!*

The man *believed* he was freezing, so strongly that his brain sent out messages that brought about his death, clinically diagnosed as due to hypothermia. "In other words," Conner writes, "there is no real or clinical difference between freezing to death by imagination and freezing to death through prolonged exposure to sub-zero temperatures."

Out of this emerges the truth that we can think ourselves into being sick or well, powerless or powerful. Nobel laureate Roger Sperry's research on the human brain indicates that positive and negative thoughts can neurologically attract similar thoughts. Conner notes that in areas where the emphasis is on peak performance, as in sports, sales, and accelerated learning, the use of *affirmations* — aimed at establishing new neurally positive bondings — is standard practice.

The Power of Inner Role-Playing

Imaging is the powerful but simple idea of seeing things, in your mind's eye or in the well of your imagination, *before they happen.* Imaging has been used for years in medicine and in all forms of research, from physics to electronic engineering. It has now become an indispensable factor in big-time college and professional sports. In business, American industry is moving ahead with concepts such as "end-state vision," in which employees mentally picture the development of a product from inception to its impact on the market.

Inner role-playing has become the rage in professional and college sports. Imagine how it might work. *Visualize* yourself catching that 40-yard pass, over your right shoulder with two defenders leaping for the ball. *See* the basketball leaving your hands in an arching shot that will mean three points and a victory in the final seconds of the game. *Watch* your bowling ball hitting just the right crease in the pins and giving you a strike at a critical point in the tournament.

Golf great Jack Nicklaus uses the same technique. He runs a mental picture of his swing, the flight of the ball, and the way it will land on the green and roll toward the hole. Nicklaus has the knack of visualizing entire golf courses. Using images, he creates strategies for each link as though he were running a pencil over a map to chart his play from the first tee to the final green.

Dr. Charles Garfield, in his book, *Peak Performers*, cites the case of pianist Liu Chi Kung, who placed second to Van Cliburn in the 1958 Tchaikovsky competition.[4] A year later, during the Cultural Revolution in China, Liu was arrested and thrown in prison. He stayed behind bars for seven years, and during that time was denied the use of a piano. Soon after his release, however, Liu was back on tour. Critics were astounded that his mastery of the piano was finer than ever.

"How did you do this?" people asked. "You had no chance to practice for seven years."

"I did practice, every day," Liu replied. "I rehearsed every piece I had ever played, note by note, *in my mind.*"

Inner role-playing lets you live through an experience before it happens. It gives you the opportunity to prepare for times of special stress, such as public speaking, an interview, or making a presentation before a group. It allows you to *see* and to *feel* what the experience will be like, in effect, pre-living it. Obviously, you need to rehearse, rehearse, and rehearse for any important performance. Your imagination has the power to make your rehearsal vivid and real, as if you were there in that stressful moment, succeeding in your task. Imaging gives you control of yourself and the situation.

Imaging also can help to prepare you for the worst. I learned early in the game that if I expected to have a long and healthy life as a pilot, I'd best learn not only how to get the most out of myself and my airplane, but also how to prepare for the totally unexpected. The fact that I am alive today is due to the habit I learned years ago, of rehearsing in my mind everything that could possibly go wrong and precisely what I was going to do about it.

Whenever I'd climb into an aircraft for the first time, I'd study the emergency fuel system, the hydraulic and electrical systems, gear let down, and so on, and I would rehearse the procedures for an emergency landing, for dealing with engine failure, fire, icing, or some other hazardous situation. I'd see the emergency happening and then would see myself going through the right procedures, over and over until I could do it automatically. When an emergency happens, often you don't have time to think.

FLAME-OUT

Over a lifetime of flying, mental rehearsal clearly saved my life at least six times. One of those occasions was on a flight from Florida to Washington, D.C. in a T-33, a two-place version of the F-80 Shooting Star jet fighter. A young captain I did not know was in the back seat. We were approaching Richmond, Virginia, when we flew into a thunderstorm at 35,000 feet, with heavy turbulence and lightning.

I took control of the aircraft, and in the process of transferring communications, the captain accidentally hit the emergency fuel switch. Immediately recognizing his mistake, he switched the fuel back to normal. The quick on-off starved the engine of fuel for an instant, and our single engine flamed out. The lights in the cockpit went out, and I was suddenly piloting a glider through a thunderstorm with no power and no lights.

This was not a wonderful moment.

Holding the flashlight I always carried in my flight suit in one hand and flying with the other, I alerted air traffic control to clear the air space below. Then all I could do was sit back and watch the altimeter unwind. Normally, you have enough battery power for one airstart, an attempt to re-ignite the engine. An airstart wasn't recommended above 20,000 feet because the air is too thin, but we needed to get out of that thunderstorm, so after falling 8,000 feet I hit the button to send fuel into the engine, and it ignited.

Soon after leveling off, the captain in the back seat panicked. Since he had control of the navigation aids, I asked him for a heading to Patuxent Naval Air Station for my let down. He wanted to send us in a wildly wrong direction, but my instincts told me he was wrong. I hit the switch to regain control of our navigation aids, located our position, and landed safely in a heavy rainstorm. The bottom line is that you have a lot better chance of making it if you're prepared in your mind. When you're thoroughly prepared, you don't come apart under stress.

THE FLYING PROSTITUTE

Another instance of mental rehearsal saving my life happened toward the end of World War II, when I was taking off in a Martin B-26 bomber to fly from Bakersfield to San Francisco. The B-26 had two engines and thin wings that didn't provide much lift but gave it a lot of speed. It was called "The Flying Prostitute" because it had no visible means of support. At the training base in Florida, the saying about it was "One a day in Tampa Bay."

At 100 degrees, the air was thin and there was no wind. Also, the runway was short for the B-26. We picked up speed, lifted off, and I was retracting the landing gear at about 150 mph, when one of the engines died. It didn't miss or sputter. It just went dead. Under the conditions, with the sensitive nature of that aircraft, I probably would have cut the good engine and bellied in, but in front of me was an oil field with holding tanks and a forest of derricks that towered above the airplane. It would have meant setting off my own Fourth of July display. Somehow I had to get above it.

The prop on the dead engine had to be feathered NOW, before the drag pulled us into a fatal yaw, but which one was it? If I feathered the wrong engine, as happened so many times, we were going straight into the oil field. Cueing on the slight yaw I had felt when the engine went out, I cranked the trim tab overhead and slammed my hand down on the red feather button for the *left* engine. It was the right choice, and slowly, slowly, the bomber climbed just high enough to clear the towers. All of this had happened in about two seconds.

Inner role-playing, frequently rehearsed, not only gave me confidence that I could handle the situation, but it also brought forth the right answers at a life-or-death moment. Instantaneous, automatic reaction saved seven lives. One of them happened to be my own.

Four Basic Steps to Inner Role-Playing

1. *Put yourself into a relaxed, but alert and receptive state,* eliminating mental and physical tensions.

2. *Gain a clear image or mental picture of precisely what you want to happen.* See it exactly as you wish it to be, whether the event is running a marathon, flying an airplane, or conducting an interview. Pre-live the event, viewing it through your mind's eye. Make it as *real* as possible. Keep all of your thoughts *positive.* Your mind will do whatever you expect it to do, positive or negative, so banish negative thoughts from your imagination. Work at it.

3. *Keep the vision alive in your mind and experience it with all of your senses.* Reinforce with your emotions everything that you see, hear, feel, and smell. The more vividly you can experience the sensations involved with the event, the more real and the more powerful it will be to you.

4. *Imbue the scene with positive thoughts and affirmative statements.* Psyche yourself up. Say, "I'm going to succeed. I absolutely glow with competence and confidence." Find whatever affirmations work for you and make them real in the present, as if they were already true. A positive outlook requires positive "self-talk." Let that little voice within you become your built-in cheerleader. That little guy can be your best friend or your worst enemy. Make sure he's solidly on your side.

The simple but powerful tool of inner role-playing is readily available to every one of us.

CHAPTER 5

THE ORGANIZING SPIRIT

This is the true joy in life, the being used for a purpose recognized by yourself as a mighty one.

George Bernard Shaw

Esprit de Corps

The heart of a first-rate fighter squadron is certainly its pilots, crews, technicians, and support people, but it is more than that. It is a force that unites all its members in one supreme goal — to accomplish the mission. It is a group spirit, *esprit de corps*, camaraderie, a sense of trust, honor, pride, and purpose. This special quality is the driving force of any great organization in the business or professional world.

I could see that spirit in the determination of Russ Christopher, who brought his P-47, "Maggie Zass," back with two cylinders shot away, almost blind from oil covering the windscreen. Or when our operations officer, Ray Elledge, was shot down near St. Lo and kept firing his .50s all the way to the ground, into the enemy forces who would confront him if he survived the crash. Fortunately, he was taken prisoner. Most of all, *esprit de corps* is a belief that every individual's contribution is important and a passionate commitment to achieving a common purpose.

Spirit is the greatest intangible of any human endeavor. Nowhere is it more evident than in athletics. Science is applied to developing athletes from a physical standpoint, but beyond that, the determining ingredient is the power of the mind. Sports psychologists are now employed at all levels of the coaching process to help athletes focus, avoid distractions, and create a positive state of mind.

In teams of any kind, from the playing field to the office, a special synergy sometimes develops to transcend individual efforts. Things click. The team acts as one, with a group consciousness in which the good of all overrides individual interests. That team has a winning edge.

This intangible element is a function of inspirational leadership, but it cannot be imposed from the top down. It arises from within and is embodied in the values, vision, and mission that permeate the corporate culture. It is evidenced in the way people interact, take responsibility, and communicate with each other. It is in the depth of their belief in common goals.

You develop spirit not by *trying* to develop it, but by laying down the fundamentals that make an organization great.

Corporate Culture

Every organization has a corporate culture, whether or not it is consciously aware of that fact. The culture is a group philosophy, a way of thinking and operating that is evident in how decisions are made and how the group interacts and communicates. The corporate culture expresses an organization's inner core, its fundamental structure and principles. Ultimately, the culture shows up in the bottom line. It can be positive or negative. It's a value-based issue.

A corporation's actions internally and externally are a mirror image of each other. If the internal culture stresses people values — listening, cooperating, developing people — the external culture will express those same values. As one marketing director put it, *"The internal culture of the company is how you treat customers externally. The culture of the company is contagious."*

The culture is like spirit. You can't see it, but you can certainly feel it. On the one hand, it can be an atmosphere of openness and creativity, where individuals are allowed to appreciate their own worth and are encouraged to grow and contribute. The group benefits from free-flowing communication and shared responsibility. On the other hand it can be a culture of "Do it because I told you to." Autocratic leadership compartmentalizes people and establishes barriers between them. It stifles the natural creativity of positive group dynamics.

> *"I am a firm believer in establishing a company culture as a way to bolster its identity as one organization. Without culture, a company lacks values, direction, and purpose. Culture, in a word, is community. It is an outcome of how people relate to one another. Communities exist at work just as they do outside the business arena. They are built on shared interests and mutual obligations and thrive on cooperation and friendship. It is up to us as leaders to remain focused and not assume that our organization is homogeneous. We need to continually share, teach, and enhance our corporate culture."*
>
> **Terry Stoneman**
> **CEO and President,**
> **Zipcom Corporation**

We once ran into a heavily negative group culture while working with an agency of the federal government. The atmosphere resembled the worst stereotype of bureaucracy: avoid taking risks, *"c.y.a."* (which means "cover your backside"), and have little concern for others and the larger purpose. Our efforts to turn it around were successful in that time and place, but in such a pervasively negative culture, making progress is like the Myth of Sisyphus — endlessly rolling a stone up the hill, only to have it roll back down again.

Corporate culture goes back to that inner core we have been saying so much about. It can't be changed superficially. *It is what you are.* If your corporate culture stinks, you have to rebuild from the foundation up.

In flying, a negative cockpit culture among the flight crew can be disastrous. You can't afford to have someone sitting in the left (pilot's) seat who thinks he's God almighty and is so busy yacking away that he doesn't have the wings de-iced again. These were events leading to a fatal airliner crash a few years ago.

I recall viewing a videotape on cockpit resource management involving United Airlines. United was a pioneer in this field, valuing concern for personal relationships as highly as technical competence. Using flight simulators, crews were videotaped as they wrestled with preprogrammed emergencies. Instructors taught crews to recognize how individual styles can create communications blocks that may cause accidents.

Typical comments during the video replay were, "My God, do I come across that way?" and the crew's response, "Yes, you can become extremely overbearing in some situations." Regardless of precisely what happens in each case, the point is clear that maintaining a positive cockpit culture, with cooperation and harmony, can literally mean the difference between life and death.

James Kouzes and Barry Posner, in their book, *The Leadership Challenge*, cite a four-year study of nine to ten firms in each of twenty industries that found that *"firms with a strong corporate culture based on a foundation of shared values outperformed the other firms by a large margin."*

- Their revenue grew more than four times faster.
- Their rate of job creation was seven times higher.
- Their stock price grew twelve times faster.
- Their profit performance was 750 percent higher.

Kouzes and Posner further relay research results of management professors David Caldwell and Charles O'Reilly that while organizational values may differ, highly successful organizations with strong cultures shared three characteristics: *"high performance standards, a caring attitude toward people, and a sense of uniqueness and pride."*

Every one of the highly successful companies we have worked with is founded on a strong, value-based culture that incorporates every facet of the company's operations, from recruiting to marketing and sales. Anything that threatens the culture threatens the company.

Rhett Linke, president of Federal Computer Services Corporation, an information technology services company in Reston, Virginia, has said that his company holds the *quality of life* as one of its highest values. A few years ago, he said, the company hired a new sales manager, and the manager picked sales people who tried to change the company and make it more like the large organizations they had come from. "Internally," he said, "our people got scared. They were afraid we were focusing on the wrong things. Some of our basic values were being questioned because of the way they were operating. Instead of surfacing issues internally so that they could be discussed, they tried to hide them." By the time the sales manager was ousted, he and his team had infected the company with a virus of doubts and fears that was threatening its long-term health.

When your operational concept leads people to empowerment, when they are truly aligned, and when your values, vision, and mission come from a deep inner core, not only is the organization doing what is morally or ethically right, but it is also practicing sound business policy. The organization will get top marks on the moral — and on the business — scorecard.

Morally, you can look at yourself in the mirror every day and know that what you're doing is honest, decent, and fair. In business terms, you are creating the kind of positive spirit that releases innovation and increases productivity. With all of your people liking what they're doing, wanting to be there, and feeling ownership of the mission, you will have a closely knit team. Everyone will know that he or she counts.

Fundamentals of Organization, Discipline, and Training

ALIGNMENT

Esprit de corps and *alignment* go hand-in-hand. If you have one, you have the other. If either is missing, the other will be absent as well. "Alignment," which will be discussed in chapter nine, describes a system of operating in which the organization functions in close harmony, like a symphony orchestra. The combination of valued team members interacting with respect and understanding for each other, and on the basis of shared values, creates a new group synergy.

The foundation for alignment and for the group culture is to bring everyone on board in setting the direction and goals. Working with a company that has had an average annual growth rate of 55 percent over the last ten years, we found that the mission and goal-setting process had become an essential means of bringing new employees into the corporate mentality. In fact, the company insists on hiring only those people whose personal values are compatible with its spirit.

Ben Clark, the company's vice president of engineering, has been with the organization since its founding and has played a significant part in its growth. He said his greatest revelation as a manager was that the key priority of his job was not to have his team install computers faster, "but to nurture the same passionate camaraderie amongst my team that had been nurtured in me over the prior months." Now he tries to teach the managers that work for him the same lesson.

Clark acknowledges that the "passion to succeed synergistically" can't be expected from everyone. The people who don't want oneness with the team don't get hired. Even though being able to hire the brightest and best engineers in the world is one of the key barriers for the continued growth of the company, Clark says, the organization remains adamant on hiring in its own image. *"If I feel that someone will not be able to learn our team-oriented culture and zealously want to add to the existing synergy, I will not hire them, no matter how technically competent they are."*

> *If you and your coworkers also possess the Organizing Spirit, spread it around and make it contagious. You'll be amazed at how much further you can travel when all of the wheels are pointing in the same direction.*
>
> **Ben Clark**

TRAINING

Training is something that organizations sometimes think they're too busy to do. In fact, they may be so busy mopping up the floor that they don't have time to shut off the water.

One of the greatest corporate challenges in this era of leanness and intense competition is simply finding the *time* to conduct training of any kind. An administrator of a health care facility acquired by a national corporation found that she no longer had time for the kind of training and team building that helped give her team the lowest turnover rate on the staff.

"All organizations have people with a lot of talent and ability," she says. "They don't have the time to help them develop."

Dealing with crises, dysfunctional families who take their frustrations out on the staff, and continual change, make it difficult even to maintain the team, let alone set aside time for leadership development and team building, says the administrator. And when she goes to a leadership workshop and gets inspired and excited, she wants to come back and share the ideas with others. "But it's a little here and a little there," she says. "It's hard to put into practice some of the things you have learned because of the demands put on you by corporate."

To me, this is the kind of short-term, bottom-line mentality that will not serve the organization well in the future. If you have no time for growth and development, you have no time for fulfilling the potential of the organization.

Training develops people resources. Picking up a sexy new piece of software and expecting it to solve problems for you could be a waste of time and money if people aren't trained to use it. Before you market a new product, you have to make sure you have the ability to install and service it properly.

Training says, "I have deep concern for you, and I want to help you grow personally and professionally." People can see that. Training is a key to building spirit.

INTERNAL BELIEF SYSTEM

Consistently, managers are concerned with improving performance, but they may overlook the fact that self-confidence or self-image, the *internal belief system*, is the generator of performance.

Allowing someone to do it himself, in his own way, is the approach most of us learned in our family lives. With my sons I would often be frustrated and want to get in and do the job myself, but that was a short-term approach. Letting them have the responsibility paid off.

In creating the Air Force tactics school in Korea, my approach could have been, "You've got to get a better handle on flying safety and cut down on these accidents," but that would have been a negative message. What worked was the positive approach. Our focus was on people, helping them become better flyers and better team members, and we worked very hard to make pilots master of their birds. The idea was not to improve the record, but to improve flying proficiency. As a consequence, the pilots felt better about themselves, which increased their performance results, and the accident rate dropped dramatically.

There is a strong interrelationship between the "doing" of training and developing confidence in one's own abilities.

DELEGATION BY NEGOTIATION

Instead of ramrodding your own ideas through, you delegate better by *negotiating*. You find the right people, lay out the problem, and say "What do you think is the best way to handle this?" You put yourself in their shoes and treat them with respect. If you allow them to come up with the ideas, you'll likely find the best and most feasible solution. They know what can and cannot be done, and the goals become theirs. Response to constant change requires an organization that is free to innovate.

INNOVATION

An environment that stresses the importance of every individual and encourages thinking, free expression, and creativity will continually produce new solutions.

On the missions we flew across the Channel from England, we would have to carry external fuel tanks. There was a glass tube in the line so the crew chief could ensure that fuel was flowing before sending a bird off on a mission. But the runway, which had been a cow pasture, was so rough that the tube would often break, shutting off the fuel from the tank.

"D" Flight Chief Harold Barlett and my crew chief, Pat Vercande, came up with a solution that was first tried on my aircraft. They took some rubber tubing from a badly shot up B-24 bomber that had come down at our base, and replaced the glass tube. It worked so well that they put it on all the birds in one flight, then the squadron, and in short order the rubber tubing became a standard for Ninth Air Force.

Team members were encouraged to think for themselves, and each felt a sense of *pride* in the end product. *Breakthrough solutions were commonplace.*

TRUST

Any time you find a high degree of esprit de corps, you automatically will have a high degree of *trust*. Mutual trust grows with individual confidence and self-esteem. Creating *esprit de corps* is impossible without the trust that allows for a free flow of ideas in all directions and a true sharing of responsibility and ownership.

Mutual Understanding

INTELLIGENCE

The left hand always has to know what the right hand is doing. As squadron commander, I wanted to fly every combat mission I could. That was the only way I'd know where the front was and where the hot spots were. That's what military (and business) intelligence is all about — information gathering and sharing.

The function of intelligence was to provide as much information as possible about the target and enemy opposition before we flew a mission. Afterward, it was to debrief every pilot, to ask, "What did you run into?" "What did you learn?" "What problems did you have?" We all needed to know the answers so that we could be prepared to meet the problem. The same is true in every walk of life today.

COMMUNICATION: THE BIG PICTURE

The corporate culture of a great organization will encourage *openness* and *communication* — among all levels, in all directions, both internally and externally. This information flow will be a part of the organizational structure, a requisite for alignment and teamwork.

The CEO of a company we work with holds a regular Monday morning staff meeting, with headquarters in other cities brought in by telephone and closed-circuit television. Once a month all of the leaders gather for a face-to-face meeting. Ensuring that everyone is interacting with everyone else is a conscious, planned effort to keep everyone informed of what everyone else is doing. It is a structured attempt to hold the Big Picture in view and avoid conflicting purposes.

When I worked on the Polaris/Poseidon/Trident missile project as a systems engineer, we were given carte blanche to look at the systems as a whole. In viewing only one major component of the system, the Command and Control guys appeared to be doing a terrific job, but when you stepped back and looked at the total picture, you could see real opportunities for improvement. Just as management by objectives will fall on its face when the long term is overlooked, shortcomings will crop up when the Big Picture is unclear.

Determination and Courage

Spirit is composed of many character traits that represent the greatest of human attributes. Among these are *determination* and *courage*.

I was commanding a Fighter Group of 75 F-86 Sabre Jets in Korea just after the Korean War when I served under an extraordinary person who for me personifies the ability to persevere against all odds. The Wing Commander was Colonel Benjamin O. Davis, Jr., the first black officer to command a high-level Air Force unit that was almost totally white. In a recently integrated Air Force he faced a unique situation and made it work. One of the famous "Tuskegee Airmen," he was later to become a lieutenant general.

Col. Davis never discussed racial issues or complained of the indignities he had suffered in his military career. It was only when I read his book, *Benjamin O. Davis, Jr., American,* that I had any idea of what he and his wife, Agatha, had been through on his solitary climb to the top ranks of the Air Force.[2]

As the only black cadet at West Point, he had been given the "silent treatment," which meant that no other cadet would speak to him for the entire four years he was there. His dream was to be a flyer, but he was rejected by the Army Air Corps, which then had no plans to create black flying units. He was advised by a general to leave the Army and attend law school. In retrospect, he believed that the general had done him a favor. "He brought out my stubborn streak," he said, and made him determined to prove his worth. Everywhere they were stationed, he and Agatha were snubbed and frozen out of social affairs by their peers and even their commanding officers.

Davis recounts these events as historical facts and without the bitterness that would have corroded other men's souls. His ordeal in rising to the rank of general tempered him like carbon steel, but it did not destroy him. Because of the depth of his character, it made him stronger. Benjamin Davis is a living example of Winston Churchill's famous admonition to never, never, never, never give up.

* * *

In the *esprit de corps* of a combat fighter squadron, extraordinary courage was a daily fact of life.

Take the young P-47 pilot who had to land while carrying two 250-lb. fragmentation bombs hung up under his wings. Although it was risky, he came in anyway. As soon as his wheels touched down, one of the bombs fell off and exploded on the runway, tearing the P-47 apart.

I ran over to pull him out, but he was riddled with shrapnel, bleeding so profusely that there was no way he could live.

"Hi, Major," he greeted me. "I guess I get the Purple Heart, don't I?"

And then he died.

* * *

Growing up during the Great Depression left me with many memories, including an unforgettable lesson in living.

A large furniture store in San Francisco, Lachman Bros., provided an inspiration for people to pull themselves out of the hole. The store had a large flashing sign that cycled through two messages. The first read, "DEPRES-

SION." The light would go out and then come on again. This time it said, "PRESS ON."

We all have ups and downs in life. But how do you get off the floor when you're immobilized? Well, you've always got a reason to get up — something you believe in or something you have to do out of necessity. That's your motivation. Then let the positive take over. Stop thinking about all the negatives in your life. Think of your strong suits and see yourself doing what you have to do. Start exercising; take action to build your own self-esteem. Make one promise to yourself and keep it, no matter what. Summon the courage to believe in yourself. As the great Alabama coach, Bear Bryant, said, "Come back and come back and come back."

Willingness to Take a Calculated Risk

Spirit implies a certain quality of *daring*, a readiness to try something new and take a chance. For a true leader, being willing to take calculated risks goes with the territory. For a great organization, encouragement to stretch the envelope, to explore and seek new ways of doing things, is a bedrock of the corporate culture.

In the fighter pilot business, I stuck my neck out and could have gotten it chopped off any number of times. One occasion was when I was director of operations for the fighter wing in Hahn, Germany, that had initially failed its readiness inspection. Laid out on a flat hilltop above the Mosel River, Hahn Air Base had a beautiful location with the lousiest weather in Europe.

The weather had been terrible for some time, preventing us from conducting some badly needed training at Wheelus Air Base in Tripoli, Libya. Those were the days before the rise of Qadhafi and his looney tunes regime. Flying conditions were great for live firing and bombing practice, but we couldn't get off the ground to get there.

With a lot of all-weather experience under my own belt, I knew that my eight hand-picked pilots could get through safely in their F-100 Super Sabres. The ceiling was nearly at zero, but I worked it out with the weather guys that at the moment of takeoff, the teletype would reflect a strange, anomalous spike to a 200-foot ceiling.

A moment or so before engine startup, the wing commander and his boss, the two-star general who commanded Twelfth Air Force, came up the stairs of the control tower. I didn't know he was on the base.

"What's up, Shook?" the general said. As I laid out my plan to get to Libya, including the fact that three nearby airbases were open and we could come down at any of them, I could hear the joyful sound of jet engines winding up. The general made no comment. He just stared at me.

High up in the control tower we were in and out of the fog. We could hear the birds taxiing, but we couldn't see them. Then the flight leader came on the radio.

"Cobra Leader. Am I cleared into takeoff position?"

I nodded, and the control tower operator gave clearance.

The general looked at me again as the first pair of F-100s ran up their engines to full power to begin the takeoff roll. Then we heard the *whump* of their afterburners kicking in. We got a glimpse of the first two birds as they shot by the control tower and disappeared into the fog. Two more flashed past, and in a minute they were all airborne.

Things were a little tense over the next two hours until we heard that all eight were safely on the ground in Libya. Everything had come up roses. If it hadn't, my head would've rolled.

I had full *confidence* in the engineering, maintenance, and communications people that the aircraft would perform perfectly. We even had a spare bird standing by, ready to roll. I had confidence in the pilots and *trusted* their squadron commander. The wing commander trusted my judgment, as no doubt did the general. Otherwise, they would have stopped me in my tracks.

It was a well-calculated risk, the kind that leaders have to take.

Those who wait for every one of the pieces to fall into place before they make a decision could well wait forever and never make a breakthrough or discovery.

CHAPTER 6

BALANCE IN TEAM BUILDING

The person who figures out how to harness the collective genius of the people in his or her organization is going to blow the competition away.
Walter Wriston, former CEO, Citibank

Practicing What You Prefer = High Proficiency

When you're doing what you really love to do, you're going to develop a high degree of proficiency. I loved to fly a fighter and became skilled in flying because I practiced, practiced, practiced what I loved to do. There was nothing I enjoyed more than taking a bird and bending it to the absolute limit of its flight ability. But if somebody is trying to do something he doesn't like, he's never going to develop that same state of high proficiency.

There's a true story I like about a little girl and a baby seal. The child had acquired a seal pup whose mother had died or abandoned it, and she cared for it so lovingly that the seal would follow her all over the house, waddling from room to room. It would sleep at the foot of her bed and even try to sing as she played the piano.

One day after the seal was nearly grown, she took it for a ride in a rowboat and then put it in the water. At first the seal was bewildered, but once its head went under, its natural instincts took over. It turned from a clumsy land animal into a graceful and fun-loving water animal. It dived and frolicked, soon caught a fish, and went wild with joy in its own habitat. After that, it looked forward to its daily swim in the lake.

When we're swimming upstream, our heads may be there, but our hearts certainly won't. We're like seals out of water, coping clumsily with an alien environment, perhaps not even knowing that a better alternative exists. Just as the seal became a creature of grace and beauty when it found its natural habitat, being where we belong liberates our potential.

The message here is to get into an arena that ties into what you like to do. Ultimately, that is where you will achieve your greatest and most fulfilling success. Doing what turns you on is also a formula for enjoying life and creating the kind of future you want.

On his 90th birthday, George Burns was asked what advice he had for young people. He said, *"Fall in love with your future."*

Work Functions in a High-Performance Team

GOOD-BYE, LONE RANGER

The days of the Lone Ranger — the entrepreneur or manager who could operate single-handedly, coming up with all the ideas and answers — are gone. The business environment of today and the future is so complex and in such a continual state of change that success depends much more upon the output of teams and work groups than on the efforts of a single individual.

The team is a *multiplier of potential.* Effective teams create a synergy that can expand the effect of the individual's efforts exponentially. The managers of tomorrow will be leaders of teams. They must understand team dynamics and interpersonal relationships and how to achieve great performance from people working together.

THE IDEAL TEAM

The ideal in team building would be to create a team in which everyone is doing what he or she does best. But there is more to it than that. The team members can't all be doing the same thing in the same way. To be effective, the team has to represent a diversity of personalities and skills. People differ not only in what they like to do and are good at, but also in the way they approach problem solving and creativity. Everybody has something special to contribute.

Teams of any kind need to be *balanced* with a variety of personality types — people with differing viewpoints and interests and skills. I have heard of an organization putting several administrators, analytical types, together in an ad hoc committee and giving them a task. Time passed, but nothing happened. They were all collecting data like crazy, but nobody knew what to do with it. For a team to carry a project through from start to finish calls for different kinds of people, each with differing interests and capabilities, playing different roles in the group dynamics.

DON'T CLONE YOURSELF

In hiring, it takes a deliberate effort to bring somebody on board who's not just the same as you. You already think like you. Why should you hire someone else who thinks like you? You should seek a *commonality of values*, of course, but you don't want clones of yourself all around you. If you're a bull in a china shop, you're going to have a lot of broken crockery. Hire and develop people who can bring to the organization the benefit of creative conflict and a diversity of operating styles and skills.

> *We write software and implement the software we write. Working on a product takes weeks, and people need quiet time to focus on that alone. We also have people who make modifications and enhancement, a job that may take an hour. Some people like long-term projects, and others are more comfortable with troubleshooting. You have to pick the right person for the right job. Analyze their personality, see that it fits well with what they do. You can't force someone from one role to the other.*
>
> *I have done a lot of coaching soccer. You can't take a defender and make him a striker. A striker is a free spirit who floats around somewhere in front. The defender has to focus on whoever's coming at him. He can't wander around. The goalkeeper is the one other unique position. This is the ultimate risktaker, the person who wants glory and is willing to take the ultimate chance, with great rewards and high liability.*
>
> *I encourage managers to go coach a sport. They can learn the same thing as here. You've got eleven or sixteen people or whatever, and you can't change them during the season. That's what you've got. The COST of bringing a new person on board is huge.*
>
> **Peter Kauffman**
> **President, M.E.I. Software Systems, Inc.**

To Create Balance

Until a few years ago, we had no truly effective means of determining what kind of role people would play on a team, and correspondingly, what kinds of roles the team needed in order to perform successfully. The system we have found to help make those crucial distinctions is nothing short of revolutionary. In our view, it provides a tool for effective team building that was never before available.

The system for achieving balance in the makeup of teams is from *Team Management Systems.* It was developed by two Ph.D.'s, Charles Margerison and Dick McCann. We have been using it successfully for nearly ten years. Margerison and McCann were intrigued by why some teams succeed and others don't, and after extensive research, they determined that the answer had to do with people doing what they liked to do and were good at — individual "*work style preferences.*"[1]

The starting point of their research was to identify key work elements. These are the kinds of tasks that need to be accomplished if a team is to be successful. They interviewed teams from many different business sectors, industry, finance, consulting, marketing, planning, and engineering. They identified nine work functions that are common to all teams, regardless of the work content. They combined these into a "Types of Work" model.

The Types of Work Model

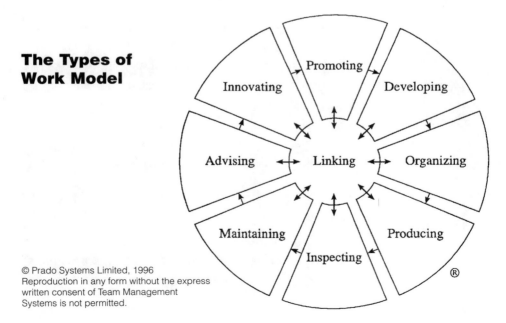

Types of Work Model

The model places eight distinct work functions in a circle around a ninth, "linking," which is the function that coordinates everything else. The functions are sequential, beginning at the 9 o'clock position:

- *Advising:* gathering information and disseminating it to others.
- *Innovating:* thinking up new products or services or ways to improve existing ones, based on the information that has been gathered.
- *Promoting:* selling the idea to the organization.
- *Developing:* making the idea work.
- *Organizing:* implementation through planning, budgeting, and scheduling.
- *Producing:* producing the product or service on a regular basis, according to standards of effectiveness and efficiency.
- *Inspecting:* a means of maintaining quality and establishing control over expenses.
- *Maintaining:* corporate support functions, such as administrative, that provide a solid infrastructure for all other work activities.

Talking with people in any of the work functions, Margerison and McCann found that those who really enjoyed their work shared common behavior characteristics. "Promoting" people, for example, were creative, while "producing" people were more practical. So they decided to look further into the relationship between the type of work and personal characteristics.

How People Behave at Work

Margerison and McCann discovered that people often behave differently at home than in the workplace. Someone who is outgoing at work, for instance, may withdraw at night in order to recharge his batteries. Since they needed to concentrate on workplace behavior, they couldn't use the highly regarded Myers-Briggs personality inventory (see chapter eight), because it produced more of a global than a work-oriented view.

They found the "psychological type" studies they needed in the constructs of Carl Jung and used them to develop a testing instrument called the *"Team Management Index."* The TMI is a sixty-item questionnaire that indicates how people prefer to work in the key management areas of *leadership, decision making, team building, interpersonal skills, organization,* and *information management.*

The Team Management Wheel

To relate the work preferences to the work functions, they conducted a study in 1988 of some 6,000 managers, asking them to describe the way they preferred to work in each of the functional areas. With this and the results of the TMI, they created the *Team Management Wheel*, which would bring both preferences and functions together. The index profile of every team member could be mapped on the wheel, indicating the team function that every individual would best perform.

Margerison-McCann Team Management Wheel

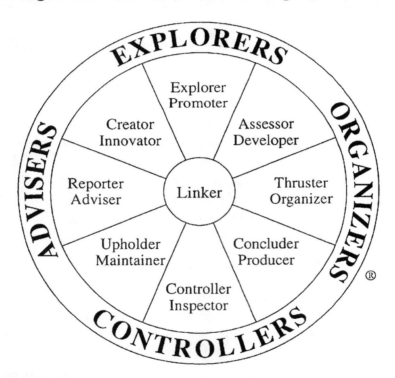

© Prado Systems Limited, 1996
Reproduction in any form without the express written consent of Team Management Systems is not permitted.

The Team Management Wheel gives dimension to the Types of Work model, adding the content of the role to the work preference. The eight work roles are again centered around the coordinating skill of *linking*, and each has two names. The first is the behavioral preference, and the second is the type of work. Thus "Concluder Producer" indicates that a person *likes* to bring things to conclusion and *does* it through producing.

Briefly, these are the eight Sectors of Work roles:

Reporter Advisers: Excellent at gathering information and putting it together so that it can be readily understood. They are patient and will wait until they have all the information before taking action. They do not enjoy conflict.

Creator Innovators: Future-oriented people who enjoy thinking up new ideas and new ways of doing things. They are independent and need to be managed with few constraints.

Explorer Promoters: Entrepreneurial risktakers who are good at taking ideas and promoting them to others. They can be persuasive and are excellent at seeing the Big Picture and generating enthusiasm. They are highly energized, active people.

Assessor Developers: They may not always think up good ideas, but they are excellent at making someone else's ideas work. Sociable, outgoing people, they enjoy looking for new markets or opportunities. They have a strong analytical approach and enjoy pushing an idea forward into a workable scheme.

Thruster Organizers: People who enjoy making things happen. They will meet conflict head-on to get things done on time and on budget. They prefer to work according to an established plan and excel at organizing people and systems.

Concluder Producers: Strong, practical people who can be counted on to carry things through to the end. Their challenge is not in dreaming up new ideas, but in a job well done. They are stable and reliable and can deliver results. They are in demand as managers.

Controller Inspectors: Quiet, reflective people who enjoy detailed work and working with facts and figures. Careful and meticulous, they have the patience to spend long periods of time on a particular task, working quietly on their own.

Upholder Maintainers: Individuals who stand by their strong personal values and have high concern for people. They prefer to work in a supportive environment and to take an advisory role in the background. They will stick by their principles and dig their heels in when their beliefs are opposed.

Responses to the index are computer-analyzed to produce a 4,000-word personal profile. Because the report reveals an individual's strengths and areas where there is room for improvement, it helps the person understand himself and others. Using the wheel and the profiles, managers and teams can see how the individual work preferences compare with the required team roles and with the demands of the job, and they can work together to improve performance.

People find that there are certain areas in which they have strengths and where they do well — and certain areas they just don't like at all and may bomb out on. Sometimes we're all forced to do what we don't like, but with a little flexibility and resourcefulness, we can carry it off. It is clear that nobody, by virtue of interest and competence, is ever going to have nines all the way around the wheel.

As we progress with the exercise, the organization finds that regardless of what it does, whether it's accounting, research and development, CAD/CAM, it has to address all of the areas on the wheel. However, all areas are not of equal importance to each organization. The overall makeup of the teams will vary according to the nature of the activity. An R&D business, for example, would be near the top of the wheel, with creativity at the head, while a straight manufacturing operation would be at the opposite side of the chart, where teams would need to take careful account of the nuts and bolts.

With the Team Management Wheel, leadership can quickly see the team's strengths and weaknesses and what roles need to be filled to make sure that all bases are covered.

Working with one organization that was just starting out some years ago, with eight people and a $600,000 per year gross, we pointed out immediately that of the eight team roles, three were going to give the company problems. On two it was cut a little bit and would bleed, but on the third it could well hemorrhage and bleed to death. The company moved quickly to cover the two lesser problems from in-house resources and brought in a new person to meet the critical challenge. Today the corporation has become an industry leader, selected for two consecutive years for the *Inc. 500* list of the fastest growing business in the nation. While there is vastly more that has gone into its success, the Team Management Wheel helped to provide it with a first-class start.

Some years ago when I joined this company, we had a large team, thirty individuals who were new employees. They were supposed to take development of a pharmaceutical product from an early stage to submission to the Food and Drug Administration. We didn't know what the composition of that team should be, what its strengths and weaknesses were. We wanted to develop commitment and task ownership.

Hal and Marilyn had a one-day seminar in which they talked about team structure and used the Team Management Wheel. Then they placed members of the team in their ROLES and showed them what their strengths and weaknesses were and gave them some suggestions on how to overcome their weaknesses. They showed them how to be more open and understanding with each other. The exercises helped them understand the channels of communication and how they could vary. The team was very young in age and for 50 percent of them, it was their first job. It helped instill good work ethics.

Today the team is still together, and it's one of the best in the company. It has won Team of the Year award several times. It was a great learning experience. I would recommend it.

Dr. Neila Nichani Smith
Medical Director and Director of Operations
A Leading Pharmaceutical Contract
Research Organization

Two Essentials of a High-Performance Team

We have seen that the first essential for achieving high performance in a team of any kind is *balance* in the roles of the various team members. If the team is out of balance or lacks coverage in specific areas, it's up to the team/organization to fill the gap, first on a short-term basis — even though someone might be required to work in an area that does not reflect their personal preference. In the long term, the goal would be to create a balanced team in which every person is in their area of strength and interest.

The second essential for a high-performance team is that the team have a high degree of *linking* skills (chapter seven). Linking was at the center of the Team Management Wheel because it is the central function that coordinates and integrates all of the other functions. Linking is a continuous process of touching all bases, within and without the organization, in order to maintain a network of communication and cooperation. Linking is often one of a team leader's major responsibilities, but it is also a responsibility of every team member.

What Does Balance Mean in Life?

We've probably all had the feeling of being burned out or pushed to the wall at some time in our lives. Or we feel that we're missing out on a lot. Time goes by and we just do the same thing, over and over. To live in a way that is complete and fulfilling, we also need to address the issue of *balance* in our personal lives.

Balance in life is about finding how to devote the attention we need to our career, family, and ourselves, when all are highly important and deserving. It is about allocating our time and energy in a way that fits our needs. Warren Bennis has commented that "True leaders lead fully integrated lives, in which their careers and their personal lives fit seamlessly and harmoniously together. Professional and private activities complement and enhance each other."[2] Attaining balance requires setting personal goals and prioritizing our relationships so that they align with the goals. To lay out personal plans and priorities, the R.O.A.D. process, which we will discuss in chapter thirteen, is the best direction-finder we have found.

The potential benefits of finding balance are to achieve Socrates' life well lived, and therefore, peace of mind. Don, to take an example, was making an excellent salary and enjoying an affluent lifestyle with his wife, a dentist who was just establishing her practice, and their three children, but his work required a lot of travel. With company downsizing, Don was moved to a new position with longer hours, leaving even less time for his family. He reached a crisis point when the children's nanny quit and he had to take leave to care for the children.

He and his wife had a serious discussion about whether or not he could quit his job and wondered if they could get by for a while on one income. Since his wife's dental practice was now flourishing, he decided to honor his value system of "family first." He established a consulting business in which he could more or less choose his hours. This would allow him to be a major player in the children's formative years. It was a tough decision that was based not on stereotypes of what we should be, but on an assessment of what would contribute most to life. For Don and his family, it was a "win-win."

Balance is not the same to every person. Each of us has to determine what balance means in our own lives. If you're a workaholic, look at yourself with your eyes wide open. If you can say, "This is what I want," in my book that's just fine. The important thing is to make your own clear-sighted judgment. Factoring in your personal mission and goals statements will help you determine the priorities in your life.

Just remember the old Arab (and Spanish) saying:

"Take what you want," God said, "and pay for it."

LINKING IN TEAMS

*The reason you don't understand me, Edith, is because
I'm talkin' to you in English and you're listenin' in dingbat.*
Archie Bunker

Coordinating and Integrating the Team

However well-balanced the team may be, it's not going anywhere if its members can't work together. Team members have to be able to hear each other and to express themselves so that they can be understood. They have to coordinate and integrate their activities if the team is going to reach its peak productiveness. Getting along with people, in families and in the workplace, isn't just a hit-and-miss proposition, a matter of having an especially gifted personality, or luck. It's a question of skill. We learn the skills of relationships all our lives. Within a team, those skills can be learned, developed, and focused.

Coordinating and integrating the activities of the team is *linking* — the second of the two essential elements of building a great team. Linking is networking, establishing channels of communication among people, and building relationships of trust and mutual understanding. Linking is a people skill. It's what pulls the team together, and therefore, it's at the hub of the Team Management Wheel. This coordinating function is one of the primary responsibilities of a team leader. But every member of the team must be aware of the skills involved and practice them actively.

Shades of Gray

In a team or with clients, we're not always dealing with someone who thinks or reacts just as we do. To establish and maintain productive relationships, we need to recognize our great diversity.

I'll never forget a training movie we were shown before combat in World War II which portrayed the psychological differences among people in responding to the stress of war. It showed a spectrum with a small group of people on each end and everybody else scattered somewhere in between. The film was in black and white and had no intent of racial overtones.

The group colored white, at one end, would not break in the face of danger, no matter what. At the other extreme was a small group represented by the color black, which would break at the first sign of pressure. The film pointed out that the great majority of people were some shades of gray — each having some degree of stability and vulnerability.

With rare exceptions, none of us is consistently on either end of the spectrum. Whether the issue concerns pressure, challenge, or trauma of any kind, we are all some shade of gray. And we are all different.

Dealing with our diversity and making it work for the organization takes continuing effort to understand ourselves and each other. Learning the skills of linking is another step in bringing diverse personalities together, and therefore, it strengthens team building.

The Skills of Group Interaction

In the Team Management Wheel, the eight roles in the outer circle are based on personality characteristics. Since these traits are the product of our inner nature, background, and experience, they essentially represent what we are and what role we find most productive in the workplace. They take a lifetime to define and, for most people, are not easily changed.

Linking, however, is not a matter of personal preferences. It is a different kind of role, based on skills of group interaction. These are skills a manager and team members can learn relatively quickly.

Essential Skills for Team Leaders

Margerison and McCann have identified linking as a vital element of team building. From their studies they report that every successful team they found had one or more people acting in a linking role.[1] Where linking skills were low, they found poor performance. A team needs people who are able to bring it together and establish effective teamwork practices. In new teams, the leader generally takes on this role. In well-established teams, everybody takes part.

We've been surprised by some of the reactions when we have asked groups to rate the linking skills in their organization on a scale of one to seven. We've almost had a couple of revolts — not about what we were doing, but about what was happening within the organization. Seeing how things *should be* revealed how bad they really were.

On the first and fundamental linking skill, *listening*, we've had people say, "Hey, nobody listens to me. I make a suggestion and that's the end of it. Nobody does anything about it. They don't tell me whether they use it or not. They don't say anything." The result, in one man's words: "I don't tell them any more."

The second crucial skill, *communication*, is also an explosive issue with many organizations. We have worked with a corporation that was literally coming apart because it insisted on retaining an operating style in which one or two people were calling all the shots. To borrow a term from the intelligence community, everyone else was "compartmentalized" and unable to see how their efforts related to the Big Picture or how team members affected each other. The problem was so easy to fix and so potentially disastrous in its consequences. The solution was for management to encourage and listen to the views of all members of the team. Making decisions accordingly let everyone know they had a hand in the final outcome.

One of the problems with many corporations is that all of the decisions are made out of the "head shed." Meanwhile, the people working with the problem are closer to it and better informed about its aspects. The majority of the time they will have useful input on finding solutions. The consequence of not consulting among people is to create tunnel vision. Seeing the whole system gives a different complexion to issues.

External, Internal, and Informal Linking

There are three kinds of linking — external, internal, and informal. Each involves a set of people skills.

EXTERNAL LINKING

In external linking, an organization builds a network of relationships outside the organization. These might include keeping in touch with clientele and distributors, tracking the competition, and working with the community. A business might want to learn about the operations of a major supplier to find out if it could get an expedited delivery, or if it would always have to plan on adequate lead time.

External linking is a bridge to the outside world of your customers and your competition. It's a means of seeking and exchanging information with those outside your organization. It's also a means of influencing others for your own purposes, which is essentially a definition of politics.

The CEO of one successful corporation in the technology sector says that he will go along with a sales representative in calling on a customer, not to close the deal, but to "validate the company at its highest level." He's there to support the commitments that the salesperson has made and to show the company flag — to say this is what we're all about and we stand by our word.

Calling on the customer is also a way of finding out more about him and about trends in the industry for strategic planning purposes. When the CEO talks to other company presidents or chief financial officers and all of them are saying the same thing, that begins to suggest strategies his company should deploy. When he's with a customer, he's trying to figure out "what keeps them up at night?" He wants to know the customer's current priorities, what direction the leadership is taking, and what the business and the company have to do. He says, "You are really understanding what is the spirit of that company." All of this is external linking.

INTERNAL LINKING

Linking internally means integrating people in a team and building good working arrangements among them. It involves keeping team members updated on important issues and creating team cohesiveness and cooperation. It requires openness, an attitude of sharing, and a commitment to the team's goals. It also requires *trust*. The most productive linking relationship is one in which people care about each other and about what they are accomplishing together. A positive, value-based corporate culture provides the best atmosphere for effective linking.

A good internal linker is excellent at allocating work, readily available when problems arise, and able to resolve problems effectively.

INFORMAL LINKING

Informal linking is done by anyone who acts as a facilitator among people and across departments to get things done. The effectiveness of a work team depends to a great extent upon the ability of its members to operate an informal network, to draw on the talents of others, and to create an ad hoc team to respond to a challenge.

In *Emotional Intelligence,* Daniel Goleman tells about a study of "star performers" by Bell Labs, the famous scientific think tank near Princeton. While the engineers and scientists at the lab all rank at the top of academic IQ scores, some emerge as stars, while others are only average in their output. The study found that what made the difference was not their IQ intelligence. It was their *emotional* IQ — their ability to motivate themselves and to work their informal networks into ad hoc teams.

The stars could make things happen smoothly because they put time and effort into cultivating good relationships with people whose services they might need. Stumped by a problem, they were able to get an answer faster because they had built a reliable network before it was needed. These informal networks are especially critical for handling unanticipated problems.

Besides mastery of the networks, Goleman wrote, the Bell Labs stars had also mastered "effectively coordinating their efforts in teamwork; being leaders in building consensus; being able to see things from the perspective of others, such as customers or others on a work team; persuasiveness; and promoting cooperation while avoiding conflicts."[2]

An informal linker is not necessarily a manager, but can be anyone who coordinates naturally as part of his or her job. The linking role can shift among team members according to circumstances.

The Eleven Skills of Linking

Team Management Systems identified some common characteristics among teams and grouped them into eleven linking skills. At the top of the list are what I consider to be the two most important — *listening* and *communicating.*

SKILL NO. 1: LISTEN BEFORE DECIDING

Studies have shown that we spend more time *listening* than in any other activity during our waking hours. Yet indications are that 70 percent of oral communication is either ignored, misunderstood, or quickly forgotten.

Listening as a skill is not taught in schools. Surveys show that while we spend 9 percent of our time writing, 16 percent reading, and 35 percent speaking, we spend 40 percent of our time listening. We take listening for granted; that is, we assume we know how to do it. We really think the power resides in *speaking*, not *listening*— it's the speaker that controls the conversation.

It's hard to listen well because: (1) we have our own agenda, (2) we're bombarded by the information age, (3) we block out what isn't useful to us, (4) our own emotional baggage gets in the way, and (5) we can be easily distracted by whatever's going on around us.

But the bottom line is this: *Most of us know that the only person really worth listening to is ME. If the other guy would just shut up, I could get on with the conversation.*

Active listening requires giving someone your physical attention. Focus completely on the speaker. Be there with eye contact and body language that says "I care," rather than "Get on with it. I'm a busy person."

You need to provide verbal feedback. Communication is only effective if the listener understands the message in the way it was intended. *Paraphrase* what you heard. Make sure you understand exactly what the person meant. For instance, imagine that you're the supervisor of a team in a computer software company, and your sales representative is telling you that you're facing tough new competition. You respond, "What I hear you saying is that the competition's making it tough for you to do your job well now. What are the problems and what can we do about it?"

Working with the federal government, we found a senior executive named Steve who prided himself on being a problem-solver and a controller of every situation in his domain. He was not fully aware that things weren't going smoothly, but his deputy, Pete, knew, and told Steve what was happening. Once Steve understood how critical the situation was, he agreed with Pete's recommendation that they seek assistance. They brought us in to help.

Given a free hand to talk to everyone, we found confusion and frustration at all levels. Miscommunication was wasting a lot of time and had severe economic and emotional costs. Steve was a master of poor listening. His leadership style was to talk, talk, talk to solve problems, but he never fully understood a problem because he did not give the other person a chance to explain it completely. Because of his style, he was essentially intimidating and unavailable to people.

When these characteristics surfaced, Steve sincerely wanted to do better and asked for my advice. I suggested that he begin to talk with everyone on the staff. A short time later he told me that he was having regular brown-bag lunches with his subordinates and things were going great!

But then I learned that at these lunches *he* was doing all of the talking. In his earnest attempt to make things better, he was actually making them worse by further intimidating the employees. I told Steve that if he wanted to communicate, he could only talk one third of the time. In the other two-thirds he had to listen.

Here is a quick list of the most important listening skills:

- Focus completely on the speaker. Be physically there.
- Keep eye contact and nod your head when appropriate.
- Give feedback by summarizing and asking questions.
- Mentally review to yourself what you hear.

SKILL NO. 2: KEEP TEAM MEMBERS UP-TO-DATE ON A REGULAR BASIS

Nothing is more important to effective teamwork than *communication*. Communication in a team is about getting people together, face to face if possible, in regular meetings — not nebulous gatherings, but meetings with an agenda and a purpose. Communication is a people skill that tells employees *what* is happening and *why*, allowing them to appreciate their role and their importance.

Face-to-face contact makes it easier to ensure that messages, both verbal and nonverbal, are understood. John is given a task, for example, and asked if he can do it. He hesitates for a moment, squares his shoulders, and bites out a terse, "Sure." However, his hesitation, body language, and tone contradict what he just said. There's a problem here. If John takes on this additional task, some other job may not get done. The team leader needs to read the clues and find out what the true story is. At the same time, John needs to be open about the conflict. "I've got responsibility for X, Y, and Z," he should explain. "Which of these tasks do you want me to do?"

Meetings should be held on a regular, planned basis, always with relevant topics. There are many kinds of meetings, depending upon the purpose. Some are formal; some are informal; some are held to share information, with decisions not always forthcoming; and others are held to set specific objectives, make decisions, and assign actions.

A useful guide in meetings in which the purpose is advising and exploring is to spend one-third of the time passing on information and the rest for feedback and discussion.

SKILL NO. 3: BE AVAILABLE AND RESPONSIVE TO PEOPLE'S NEEDS

Team members need to feel that their leader cares about what they are doing. Being available and responsive to their needs is a linking skill that allows you to keep in touch with what is going on and provide guidance where you can. This does not mean being too involved on every little problem. That constitutes micromanaging and is usually a negative.

Make sure that if you announce an open-door policy, people feel welcome to walk through the door. If when team members come in, you pick up the telephone, tap your pencil on your desk, check your watch, or in some other way make it clear that people are wasting your time, they probably won't come back. Make steady eye contact, concentrate on the person, and listen to what you're being told. The issue is important, or the person wouldn't be there.

Don't try to handle important issues on the run. Set time aside for people to see you, give them your full attention, provide feedback, and take action, if appropriate.

SKILL NO. 4: DEVELOP A BALANCED TEAM OF ADVISERS, ORGANIZERS, CONTROLLERS, AND EXPLORERS

Successful team managers, however different their approach, tend to agree that one of their main purposes is to put together a winning combination of people who are working together to achieve team objectives. If the team is unbalanced, it may leave crucial functions unattended to. For example, a team of Controller-Inspectors will be good at detailed, accurate work, but they may not be able to see the Big Picture and develop new ideas. A team must have people who represent the four major areas of the Team Management Wheel.

SKILL NO. 5: ALLOCATE WORK TO PEOPLE BASED ON THEIR CAPABILITIES AND PREFERENCES

Remember the little girl and the seal. We do our best when we're in an area of our natural affinity. But that doesn't mean we have an excuse for not doing something outside our preference, if it is part of our role and job responsibility. To improve the team, the leader has to look at work *and* preference.

A successful manager I know sent a memo to his engineering staff some years ago listing nine aspects of engineering that were being performed in the company. He said, "You tell me which of these really turn you on, and we'll blend them into your work as best we can." He didn't say he could put everyone in the job of their choice. "But I guarantee you, " he said, "I'll do the best I can today, and on a longer-term basis, if you're performing right, you will be in the work area you want." The restructuring started right away, and since then his staff has grown considerably. His plan not only worked in the short term, but it was the foundation for building a staff that today has no equal in their area of operations.

SKILL NO. 6: ENCOURAGE RESPECT AND UNDERSTANDING AMONG TEAM MEMBERS

Respect for the other members of the team depends upon understanding the special skills each person brings to the job. Once people understand the variety of functions necessary for a team to perform its tasks, they begin to recognize the strengths of other individuals. Ideally this leads to mutual respect and improved cooperation and performance.

Social activities involving the team, from having lunch together to planning outside events, also promote understanding. Mike Vance, former head of Disney University, says in his book, *Think Out of the Box*, that "Despite what bean counters and bottom liners say, celebrating and socializing are important elements in the creative process." Walt Disney said, "*Socializing is a key element of the creative process; eating and drinking are part of the formula.*"[3]

Vance further says that as interdependence among workers increases, a spirit of cooperation in the workplace becomes more and more necessary. "Attitude" doesn't cut it. "No matter what you do," he says, "cooperation and interaction with other humans and increasingly sophisticated technology is essential to success."[4]

SKILL NO. 7: DELEGATE WORK ASSIGNMENTS THAT MAY BE A BETTER MATCH WITH TEAM MEMBER PREFERENCES AND ABILITIES

Discussing, as opposed to directing, is the best way to find the right match between job tasks and team member capabilities. Reviewing the prospective assignment with team members helps to identify those people who have the best interests, skills, and enthusiasm for the task.

Effective delegation, however, depends upon the training, nourishing, and empowering steps we discussed in chapter one, "Valuing People." The object is to bring people along, building their competence and confidence as you go, until you can *trust* them to do the job.

SKILL NO. 8: SET AN EXAMPLE AND AGREE ON HIGH QUALITY STANDARDS WITH THE TEAM

On every one of the dive-bombing missions I led, I was always down on the deck where it was hot. I never flew "cap," which meant to orbit high overhead, watching for enemy fighters. As a leader, my job was to be with my pilots and to take the same risks they did. Some squadron commanders flew cap whenever they could. They set an example, but it might not have been the one that would best motivate their team.

The team leader acts as a role model and is responsible for setting the example for the team. In a self-directed team, all members have to accept that responsibility. No matter what our position is on the team, we set an example by our behavior. Team members note our actions and attitudes and form their own opinions of how much respect we have for the team, its mission, and its members.

SKILL NO. 9: SET ACHIEVABLE TARGETS WITH THE TEAM, BUT CREATE CHALLENGES FOR THEM TO IMPROVE PERFORMANCE

The old saying, "nothing succeeds like success" is fundamental in developing high-performing teams. If team members believe that they are winners, they will be. If they believe they are losers, they will blame the system and become alienated.

As I have stressed, it is important to involve team members in setting goals, since then they will more likely try to achieve them. The goals need to be challenging, but not so lofty that the team is disheartened or doomed to fail. It is better to achieve a modest success and build on it, step by step, than to set the bar too high.

SKILL NO. 10: COORDINATE AND REPRESENT TEAM MEMBERS

It is important for all team members to know what everybody else, including the leader, is doing at any time. This linking skill includes internal coordination, external coordination, and representation.

Since teams usually have to work with other teams, at times a key task of the manager is to represent or, in some cases, defend the team. Morale, as well as gaining necessary resources to get the job done, may depend on how well the leader carries out the representation role.

SKILL NO. 11: INVOLVE TEAM MEMBERS IN THE PROBLEM SOLVING OF KEY ISSUES

To get people committed to implementing a solution, get them involved in the problem at an early stage. Communicate your ideas and seek their views. Draw them into the process and make them responsible participants.

Discuss controversial issues at an exploratory meeting where no decisions are made. A decision meeting can be set later. Weld the team together through facilitating and communicating. Continue to review goals and strategies and always look for a better solution or a way to improve.

How do you incorporate these eleven linking skills into your group culture? One way is to take each skill and make it a focus of your team for a specified time period. Focus on one a month or no more than two a month. You don't necessarily have to do this in order, or even cover all eleven. Once you have identified the areas that are of highest priority to you and need your most urgent attention, concentrate on them. Post the current skill and discuss its issues in your team. Define what acceptable and nonacceptable behavior are in those areas.

For one government agency I suggested taking one skill a month and making it the theme for group focus. The agency ended up doing two a month, starting with listening and communicating — the two that are *always* at the top of the list.

Linking to Solve Problems

When we were working through the ORI problems of the 50th Fighter Group in Hahn, Germany — in developing and checking on nuclear and conventional weapons release procedures — we had to ask, "Where did the instruction come from before it landed with us?" We needed to gain a clear definition of our responsibilities. We went all the way up to Headquarters, U.S. Air Force, Europe in Wiesbaden and to 12th Air Force Headquarters and its NATO counterpart in Ramstein.

At our own level we linked with all of the key people involved at the Fighter Wing Command Post. We looked at the major recipients of the release order, including Victor Alert, which was a guarded area enclosed by

The Linking Skills Jigsaw

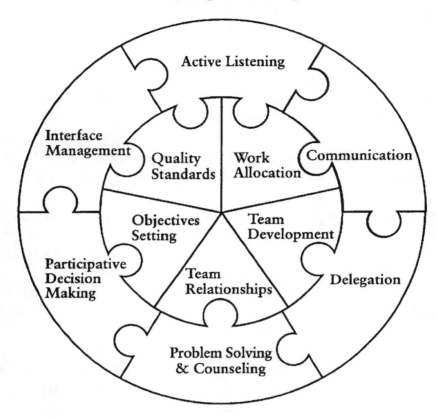

barbed wire, where the F-100s were ready to launch within fifteen minutes. We networked with all of the secondary commanders, with engineering and armament in three squadrons to rebuild our release procedures. The linking was what pointed to the extraordinary complexity of the procedures.

When we had rewritten our guidelines, we coordinated again to check them out with the higher headquarters and then put the system to a test.

The key was to exchange information and find out the best way to proceed. We couldn't have done it without linking.

CHAPTER

REINFORCING TEAMWORK

Work as a team player. The game is neither won nor lost by one person, but is rather a composite of the group effort.
Donald E. Petersen

The First Leadership Principle

I learned many leadership principles when I was leading a squadron into combat in the skies over Europe. One of the first and most important was *the absolute necessity of teamwork* in accomplishing the mission. Each man in the squadron was as important as the next one. This was true from larger sections such as engineering, armament, and communications, to "Rip Cord" Bunch's small parachute shop, on which our lives literally depended. Every pilot had to stay in formation and key on the leader. There was no room for prima donnas.

Teamwork got us into the air and brought us home. In all my flying and all the hits my airplane took, the two occasions when we came closest to not making it were on that B-26 takeoff into a forest of oil derricks and on a strafing run over France when the other members of the flight became my guardian angels.

A Wing and a Prayer

It was two days after D-Day. We had completed our dive-bombing mission, and on the way back, I sent twelve aircraft home and took my lead flight of four planes to attack a German armor concentration that we had seen on the way in. We were heading home at about 275 mph, flying at ten to twenty feet above the ground to avoid enemy fire, when near Caen I saw flashes from an enemy antiaircraft gun at my 10 o'clock. I popped up to get a good bead on the guy and turned into him, firing my guns. I got him just as he got me.

BLAM! A cannon shell exploded on my right wing, and the P-47 flipped on its side with the wingtip nearly touching the ground. I grabbed the stick with both hands and yanked it with all my strength to the left, fighting the wing slowly up to level. More than a little shaken, I could see what had happened. The explosion had torn a hole in the wing and had knocked open the three-foot door that gave access to the guns, which was acting as a huge dive brake. One of the .50s was hanging out, along with snarled belts of ammunition.

My speed dropped to a max of 150 mph, and since I was a sitting duck, the other three pilots moved up into a protective cover as I hugged the ground. I was just beginning to think I might make it home when I hopped over a hedgerow, and there twenty feet beneath my wings were massed tanks, trucks, and guns from a German panzer division. The German soldiers stared at me, open-mouthed, but since they were as surprised as I was, nobody opened fire.

I pulled up over the barrage balloons on the Normandy beachhead and crossed the Channel to England, with my teammates checking my badly damaged aircraft and guiding me in. As the wheels touched down I breathed a sigh of relief. It had been a long day, but it wasn't over yet.

Just then the right landing gear collapsed and my wing hit the ground. With no control over the aircraft, I began skidding off the runway at well over 100 mph. I was heading straight for the control truck. At the last minute, the big fighter somehow slid past the truck and stopped in the field.

I thought I'd bought it back there over Caen when the wingtip was going to hit the ground. But teamwork had brought me home. Maybe that and the grace of God.

Teams — The Primary Work Unit

Teamwork is even more important in today's business environment of tough competition, continuous change, and technological complexity than it was then. Of necessity, cooperating in teams has become the primary mode of getting work done.

Peter Drucker has coined the term "knowledge worker" to indicate the direction in which the American workforce is moving. Knowledge workers add value to information, whether it is in market analysis or computer software. Drucker points out that these workers' expertise is so highly specialized that to be productive their efforts have to be coordinated as part of a team. Drucker says that in this situation, "teams become the work unit rather than the individual himself."[1]

Pulling People Together

Some people try to lead by throwing their weight around, which usually ends up with disastrous results — if not immediately, at least down the road. Degrading people and reading them the riot act does not solve problems. It only creates new ones. Instead of dealing with the problem at hand, you'll have your people spending their energy trying to cope with *you.*

You can pull people together in two ways: by listening, learning, and building on relationships; or by acting as if you're the only one who has the right answers. In the first approach, they'll be on your side, pulling with you. The second approach also will unite them — against you. Real team building creates a positive relationship of cooperation and shared purpose, which provides the fertile ground for innovation. A team united against you may do exactly what you tell it to do, but it will do nothing more. It might even bite back.

I saw an extreme example of this attitude when our squadron was sailing for England in 1944. We were in a convoy of about thirty ships, on board a British vessel, the Sterling Castle. A first sergeant who was responsible for KP, clean-up details, and emergency procedures was bent on motivating people through fear. He pushed them around as if he were handling a cage of brainless wildcats. He was just plain nasty.

Life was hard enough without having to worry about both the enemy and a cantankerous sergeant. Word soon got around that if he didn't watch his six o'clock position and ventured too near the rail one night, he'd have a long swim home. The convoy, which included an American light cruiser, destroyers, and British corvettes, was moving fast and couldn't stop, so the sergeant probably would have ended up in Davy Jones's locker.

An adjutant with both maturity and true leadership talent saw that the situation was getting dangerous. He called the first sergeant in and laid out the facts. I don't know exactly what he said, but it worked. The sergeant did a quick turnaround, and the men could go back to fighting one war at a time.

Diversity and Creative Conflict

Managers often tend to hire people who think and act just as they do. Warren Bennis, in *Why Leaders Can't Lead,* diagnosed this as Richard Nixon's Achilles' heel.[2] Nixon couldn't see what was wrong with his attitude of being above the law, because there was no one in the White House who didn't in some way mimic his thinking. He surrounded himself with people who were essentially clones of his own moral perspective.

A healthy work team will thrive on *creative conflict,* with differing opinions continually competing in the marketplace of ideas. The team will reflect the growing diversity of gender, race, and educational background, drawing on the individual strengths of each. To be truly effective, it will also incorporate differing personality types. Differences in the way we see, think, and feel are the source of creative conflict.

This is not necessarily a comfortable goal. We all think the world would run a lot better if everyone could simply see things the way we do. But it is these different approaches and individual ways of seeing things that produce innovation.

Business consultant Ichak Adizes, speaking at an *Inc. 500* conference in Los Angeles, said that if you want to build a successful company, you need a complementary team. If you have the wrong team, all you get is negative conflict. Companies need what he calls "family energy," which is characterized by healthy conflict and diversity of opinion. *"When you eliminate conflict, you eliminate change,"* Adizes says. The trick is how to make conflict constructive.[3]

Myers-Briggs: Understanding Personality Types

It is futile to try to get people to think and act exactly alike, because the differences among them are built in. Attempting to sculpt people into our own likeness is doomed to fail.

A tool that is widely used today to help us understand our "type" of personality — the way we like to operate in the world — is the *Myers-Briggs Type Indicator*®. This personality profile also helps us understand others and, therefore, is a significant factor in strengthening relationships and team building.

The fundamental premise of Myers-Briggs is that people are different, and that the differences are *good.*

The Myers-Briggs system is based on the studies of psychologist Carl Jung. Differing with predecessors such as Freud, Adler and Sullivan, Jung declared that people are different in fundamental ways, even though they are all driven by the same multitude of "archetypal" instincts. Jung concentrated on each individual's preference for how best to *function* to maintain integrity with one's core values and adapt to the external world at the same time.

With a knowledge of your own Myers-Briggs profile and that of your teammates, you can better understand how each person approaches a task and interacts with others. Productively managing human relationships depends upon being able to appreciate the various strengths and blind spots represented in the group.

This chapter provides an introduction to the Myers-Briggs types, but it is not intended to be a full-scale treatment of the system. References for further study are listed in the Notes.[4]

The Basic Personality Types

The Myers-Briggs Type Indicator® (MBTI) is a series of questions that ask how you *prefer* to do things in life. For instance, would you rather be in a busy workplace with problems bombarding you every minute, or do you work better alone, with time to contemplate? Would you rather go to a party or stay home and read a book? Coming at personality traits from several different directions creates a composite picture of your likes and dislikes. But remember, Myers-Briggs is a profile of your *preferences,* not a description of all that you actually do.

The test classifies people according to their dominant tendencies in four categories:

E or **I** = **E**xtraversion or **I**ntroversion
S or **N** = **S**ensing or **IN**tuiting
T or **F** = **T**hinking or **F**eeling
J or **P** = **J**udging or **P**erceiving

Your four preferences are expressed in a four-letter code that describes your personality type. For example, you might be an ESTJ or an INFP. Your personality will combine qualities of *all* four (letter) types, and the profile will characterize your style of perceiving and deciding and acting. ESTJ indicates a person who tends to relate to the External (E) more than to the internal world, who prefers to deal with information by Sensing (S) over intuiting, who makes decisions by using Thinking (T) more than feeling, and who prefers to deal with external realities in a Judging (J) more than in a perceiving way.

Even though in a given individual one letter may represent a preferred style of behaving, characteristics of the opposite letter may sometimes be evident. For instance, an extravert may sometimes need solitude. A sensing person, who is mainly a "nuts and bolts" type, may have flashes of intuition. Growth in personal awareness and competence depends heavily upon our being able to coax out the less pronounced of our tendencies to help balance our natural preferences.

Extraverts put energy into interacting with people and things outside themselves. They tend to be talkative and engaging, people who tend to initiate contact, want to "put things on the table," clarify ideas by talking them out. *Introverts*, by contrast, spend much more time and energy reflecting on ideas and processes by themselves. They also tend to need more privacy and time alone than extraverts. Watch their boundaries! They'll not want you to step over certain lines and intrude on their space.

Sensors like to rely upon their five senses — smell, sight, hearing, touch, and taste. They like concrete reality. They tend to be good at understanding mechanical operations, at tinkering with machinery and fixing it. Their opposite, *Intuitives*, are far less into the nuts and bolts. They like blue-sky hypothesizing: "What if we tried such and so?" They base much of their action on gut instincts, hunches, and creative thinking.

Thinkers put great stock in using logic and being "objective" when making decisions. They just want "the facts," and they value consistency and fairness. They love to analyze puzzles in almost mathematical fashion, identify gaps, and fill in the missing pieces. *Feelers*, on the other hand, go with their emotions. They may endorse what a thinker would call an irrational course of action just because "it feels right."

Judging types like order and predictability. They don't always realize that there may be shades of gray. They like everything tied up in a nice, neat package. ***Perceivers*** are your basic "go with the flow" types. They cherish spontaneity, openness, and adaptability. They can shift positions in the middle of a discussion if they suddenly see a favorable aspect to something or get some new information.

Our Preferred Way of Acting

The Myers-Briggs type categories can be put together in sixteen different combinations. The table below gives the order of preferences (relative strengths of influence) of each of the sixteen types. No combination is really "better" than any other.

Order of the Preferences for Each Type

ISTJ	ISFJ	INFJ	INTJ
1. Sensing	1. Sensing	1. Intuition	1. Intuition
2. Thinking	2. Feeling	2. Feeling	2. Thinking
3. Feeling	3. Thinking	3. Thinking	3. Feeling
4. Intuition	4. Intuition	4. Sensing	4. Sensing
ISTP	**ISFP**	**INFP**	**INTP**
1. Thinking	1. Feeling	1. Feeling	1. Thinking
2. Sensing	2. Sensing	2. Intuition	2. Intuition
3. Intuition	3. Intuition	3. Sensing	3. Sensing
4. Feeling	4. Thinking	4. Thinking	4. Feeling
ESTP	**ESFP**	**ENFP**	**ENTP**
1. Sensing	1. Sensing	1. Intuition	1. Intuition
2. Thinking	2. Feeling	2. Feeling	2. Thinking
3. Feeling	3. Thinking	3. Thinking	3. Feeling
4. Intuition	4. Intuition	4. Sensing	4. Sensing
ESTJ	**ESFJ**	**ENFJ**	**ENTJ**
1. Thinking	1. Feeling	1. Feeling	1. Thinking
2. Sensing	2. Sensing	2. Intuition	2. Intuition
3. Intuition	3. Intuition	3. Sensing	3. Sensing
4. Feeling	4. Thinking	4. Thinking	4. Feeling

Note for Introverts

Remember, Introverts are more likely to show their #2 (auxiliary) preference to others because their #1 preference is used mainly inside, in their favored introverted world.

In MBTI terms, the order of preferences for the ESFJ is:

Dominant	=	1. Feeling
Auxiliary	=	2. Sensing
Tertiary	=	3. Intuition
Inferior	=	4. Thinking

Of the middle two preferences (SN and TF), one of these four functions is our preferred way of acting in the world. This is called our *dominant* function. Another function that helps out and supports the dominant is our *auxiliary* function. These two preferences help provide balance to the personality. Our third choice is called the *tertiary* function. Our fourth, the *least preferable*, is always the opposite of the dominant.

My dominant (or primary), for example, is Feeling, which comes on so strong that it tends to wipe out Thinking, the exercise of logic. My wife Marilyn's Intuiting is extremely strong; she uses this function to take in information and will often discount sensory data. Your great strengths are with your dominant and auxiliary. The other two functions are of lesser importance.

No combination is really "better" than any other — better for certain work roles, yes, but not better in an overall sense.

TJ Decision Makers: Product vs. People

If you look at the makeup of business leaders and decision makers on a worldwide basis, you find a predominance of TJs — those whose predominant characteristics are Thinking and judging. This is an observation made by Sandra Krebs Hirsh, a leading authority on Myers-Briggs, in her latest book, *Work It Out.*[5] Similarly, a study by Ben Roach in *The Journal of Psychological Type* showed that the four TJ types (ISTJ, INTJ, ESTJ, ENTJ) represented up to 87 percent of all organizational decision makers.[6] TJs like to take charge. With their dominating characteristics of Thinking and Judging, these managers have a preference for order, structure, planning, and control.

What they tend to overlook are the qualities of *Feeling.* These are the areas that have to do with concern for people and their needs and wants, and with values and interpersonal relations. Instead of nurturing and encouraging people as their greatest resource, the TJ leaders may focus heavily on what Sandra Hirsh calls "an unbalanced pursuit of the product at any cost to people or the environment." They concentrate on task accomplishment at the expense of relationships.

Each of the four TJ types has Feeling as their third or fourth function. Since the fourth function is the least preferred and the opposite of our dominant function, it tends to become our weak link. As in so many facets of life, what is needed here is balance. This means to balance Thinking with Feeling and Sensing with Intuition.

Balancing the functions takes conscious and repeated effort. The heavy TJs need to practice listening to others, taking others' opinions and feelings seriously, and factoring their ideas into decision making. They need to appreciate and practice the qualities of praising, teaching, and coaching and of organizing people and tasks harmoniously so that employees can actually take pleasure in what they do at work.

As I have mentioned, the function I use most is Feeling. My second strongest function is Intuiting. My tertiary function of Sensing ties in well with my flying and systems engineering experience. As my short suit is with Thinking, I make a special effort to focus on that area whenever the issue involves business. I do my best to bring it into balance with Feeling.

TJ types should do the opposite: bring Feeling into balance with Thinking. And although we know of many CEOs, directors, and team leaders who have developed this balance to a fine degree, there are many others who do not trust and only rarely use skills related to Feeling. Conversely, those who apply only Feeling at the expense of Thinking are just as badly off. They risk being run over at every turn.

As a final point, remember that Myers-Briggs sorts for preferences; it does not measure behavior. We all do what we have to do on a daily basis. We *rise to the occasion* and put forth the kind of behavior that is called for, even if it's not altogether natural. Responding intuitively to the situation in the right way is a big part of being effective with other people.

Know Personality Types for Better Understanding

Pin down your own Myers-Briggs combination and understand how *you* tend to think and act. With this understanding you will find that you are much better equipped to read other people's personality tendencies and to allow for the differences they represent.

I have been in organizations where people were just butting heads. After they saw the results of the Myers-Briggs Indicator, I heard remarks such as, "Charlie, I see you in a whole different light now." "So that's what the problem has been." What one person had previously considered "crazy" or "stupid" on the part of someone else now made sense, given an understanding of that person's personality type.

While Myers-Briggs contributes to balance in team building, it also helps create an atmosphere of understanding and cooperation in which team members are able to communicate more effectively.

Peter Kauffman, president of M.E.I. Software Systems, Inc. in Reston, Virginia, says that his company works with clients who want high tech but aren't particularly literate in technology. His customers depend on M.E.I. to support them in stressful situations. In fact, he says, it's a very stressful business. *"Man and machine aren't talking to each other,"* Kauffman says. *"They never have and they never will. They're fighting all the time."* To take the stress out of the business, you have to work on the level of personal relationships, both internally and externally.

However, Kauffman continues, high-tech people are experts in writing software and often are not people-oriented. They are bright, high producers, but often impatient and not good teachers and mentors. The remedy was, first, to apply the Myers-Briggs process to build understanding with people about themselves and their fellow workers. His employees have become more effective with people, Kauffman says, and "learning how to understand each other's characters and personalities." They also worked on team building, to bring people from the point at which they need a lot of supervision to where they can operate independently. M.E.I. started with the management team and then went out to the staff in general.

The company has moved from creating project teams on an ad hoc basis to a system in which the teams stay together for successive projects, compete against each other, and gain a sense of ownership for the project and for the customer. "The real winner," Kauffman says, "is the customer, who is dealing with somebody who has a vested interest." The system has been in place for a year and a half and has brought a tremendous improvement in the spirit of the teams and the success of the company. The success can be measured in tangible profit increases.

Loyalty and the Bottom Line

In the companies we have dealt with closely over the years, turnover is running near zero. This is true, to a great extent, because the leaders make a serious commitment when they hire an employee, and the employee makes a serious commitment to the company. The leadership goes to extraordinary lengths to make sure that the new hire will be compatible with the corporate culture. Once the individual is on board, the company provides every opportunity for growth and success.

The result is a relationship that strengthens with time.

Team building is a two-way street. A certain commitment is expected from both the leader and from the team members. This commitment is a relationship of *trust* between people, in which both owe the other a responsibility. In a team, whether the outcome is success or failure, it belongs to everyone. Everybody is in it together, for better or worse. They have good reason to form a common bond.

Instinctively, a number of world-class business leaders have realized that building *loyalty* among their employees, customers, and suppliers was key to long-term success. Now a powerful recent book spells that out: *The Loyalty Effect*, by Frederick F. Reichheld.[7] The author is director of Bain & Company, a worldwide strategy consulting firm headquartered in Boston.

The study came out of work by Reichheld and colleagues at Bain as they struggled to make sense of striking disparities in performance and growth among companies they were researching in the insurance industry. Why did some have such superior earnings, when capitalization, knowledge and intellectual capital among the firms were so similar?

A closer look led the consultants to discover the critical value of an important variable: *Loyalty*. The highly successful firms in the study had an unusually strong rate of retaining *employees* — and *customers*. Similarly significant was the loyalty of those who had *invested* in each firm. What was more, the three levels of loyalty seemed to be linked. Reichheld treats his own employer, Bain & Company, as a case in point, observing:

In my nearly twenty years at the firm, I have seen it grow from one small office on Boston's waterfront into a company of fifteen hundred employees spread across twenty-three offices around the globe. In my opinion, the key to the firm's success has been its loyalty to two principles: first, that our primary mission is to create value for our clients, and second, that our most precious asset is the employees dedicated to making productive contributions to client value creation.

Whenever we've been perfectly centered on these two principles, our business has prospered. Our most difficult times have been those few periods when we inadvertently drifted off center. In each such instance, however, the reaffirmation of our loyalty to primary principles produced a remarkably swift return to the path toward growth, profit, and lasting value.

In his study, Reichheld profiles companies that are household names for stability and reliability, such as John Deere & Company, the farm equipment maker; State Farm Insurance Company; Chick-Fil-A, the fast-food franchise; MBNA, one of the world's largest credit card companies; and Leo Burnett, the high-flying advertising agency.

The industries represented in this group are quite diverse, and so are the management styles and personalities of the firms' top people. It's on the level of *values* that the companies take on a similar look. And all these companies, according to Reichheld, have made conscious and energetic efforts to build loyalty, among both customers and employees. "Loyalty" — despite stories in the business press to the contrary — "is by no means dead," writes the author of *The Loyalty Effect*. "It remains one of the great engines of business success."

CHAPTER

ALIGNMENT

The core of a great organization is with its MVP Alignment:
the alignment of organizational and individual
Mission — Values — Players

Loose Cannon

The term "loose cannon" comes from the days of square-rigged warships. When a cannon broke its moorings in high seas, it would race back and forth across a pitching deck — two tons of brass or iron smashing into bulwarks and masts, running down any sailor who couldn't get out of the way.

An organization that has not achieved *alignment* is like a fifty-gun frigate with its cannons loose and ready to roll in every direction. It's a disaster waiting to happen. No team can share a positive, productive spirit if its members are careening off in different directions, conflicting with and canceling each other out.

Alignment: A Spirit of Shared Purpose

Alignment is a relationship of cooperation and trust among people. It is a relationship in which each member of the team is committed to the mission and goals of the organization — because every team member has had a hand in developing the organization's purpose and direction. Based on common beliefs and values, alignment includes understanding and respect among all members of the team.

It is a sense of shared purpose that creates a new synergy — a highly spirited environment of creativity and innovation.

There will always be problems, but in a properly aligned team everyone will work together to develop solutions. Solutions become everyone's business.

The Coordination of Aerial Acrobatics

I like to compare an organization with true alignment to a team of fighter pilots performing acrobatics. Take for example, the barrel roll. The airplane slowly banks upward until it's upside down and then continues on around until it has righted itself. In formation flying, the lead pilot's actions have to be smooth and coordinated, and each pilot in the formation must follow him perfectly. It's as graceful as an aerial ballet.

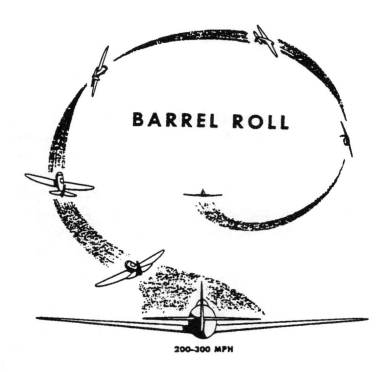

BARREL ROLL

200–300 MPH

I have rolled nearly every aircraft I have ever flown, including a DC-3 "Gooney Bird" and a Martin B-26 bomber, sometimes with a fighter on my wing. The key word is *coordination*.

In the *barrel roll*, you're creating maybe two and a half G's of gravity — enough force to keep passengers in their seats and coffee from spilling. It's like swinging a bucket of water over your head so that not a drop falls out. Your wingmen will have to coordinate their every move with yours. The pilot on the outside of the formation has to give his engine a little more power, while the pilot on the inside has to slack off a bit. The leader has to maintain a steady, even rate of roll while his teammates watch him closely to stay in alignment.

The *slow roll*, on the other hand, is an uncoordinated maneuver in which the aircraft rolls 360 degrees around a pivot point, similar to turning a chicken on a barbecue spit. If the pilot and passengers aren't strapped in, they're going to bounce around inside the airplane like ping pong balls.

These two maneuvers can be likened to an organization's operating style. Barrel rolling is cooperative and not confrontational. Managers and employees are operating in sync, with their strengths and abilities working together synergistically. It's a combined effort, an integrated process accomplished around the central point of values, vision, and mission. In contrast, the slow roll is an individual, rather than a team action. In fact, it's dangerous to attempt in close formation. This is the go-it-alone, prima donna, high-risk approach. In organizational terms, the slow roll signifies an operation that is rough, unaligned, and uncoordinated — a disaster waiting to happen.

A team in the corporate or organizational world that is performing together like the Air Force's crack Thunderbirds or the Navy's Blue Angels will be tightly knit, anticipating every move, each member knowing in advance of major tasks facing the team or individuals. Everyone is coordinated with and sensitive to the other members of the team. Together they act as one, a single unit.

This is no ordinary work relationship. But it is characteristic of the best, the great performers. Stephen Covey has noted that people begin their lives being dependent and then evolve to a level of independence. However, he points out, there is a higher level, which is *interdependence*.[1] To evolve to that level is to weld individuals into a team with a single passionate spirit aimed at achieving a shared goal.

A Relationship Based on Trust

A high level of *trust* — in each other, in the team as a whole, and in the leader's ability to show the way to success — is necessary for the development of alignment, which is the highest path toward turning mission and goals into reality. Trust is a measure of character. It is commitment with honesty, loyalty, and integrity. These are the traits of all-weather players.

Following the Persian Gulf War, every one of the major American military commanders said that the key to operational success had been trust. The overall commander, General Norman Schwarzkopf, said, "I built on trust among my components because I trusted them."

The naval commander said the component commanders shook hands and said, "'We're not going to screw this up; we're going to make it work.' And it did."

The Air Force commander said, "Trust was the key factor… there was no room for prima donnas."

Finally, the Marine commander commented, "The notion of trust may convey even more than teamwork. It's critically important that you have trust, especially at the commander level."[2]

How do you build trust? The basic truth is that *to give trust generates trust*. People respond in kind.

Alignment is a *relationship business*. To me a relationship means, basically, the way you get along with other people. It is how you relate to the boss, your peers, and those who work for you. It is a high degree of cooperation both internally and in the external operations of the organization. The ideal is to be as helpful, open, and supportive as you possibly can. In teams, hierarchies don't work. The basic values in creating positive group interaction are cooperation and consideration for others. Everybody's in this together. Every member of the team shares a common vision and purpose. The task is to create an environment in which the ideal becomes the norm.

Ichak Adizes has observed that an organization at its peak is integrated by a relationship of *mutual trust and respect*.[3] In operational terms, trust comes from the recognition that "at least in the long run, people share a common interest." Respect is when you recognize the other person's right to be different. You don't have to agree with that person, but to respect him or her, you will listen and learn. Mutual respect is an understanding and appreciation of another's strengths and weaknesses.

A strong relationship of mutual trust and respect should not only exist within the organization, but should also be extended to everyone you deal with on the outside: suppliers, distributors, service providers. A peak organization is fully integrated, both internally and externally.

As in a marriage, workplace relationships are continually evolving and changing. However, the most important component of a successful marriage is something that does not change — a deep and fundamental sharing, a basic agreement on common values and beliefs. Happy couples have much the same view of life because their values are similar. When they meet someone for the first time, they intuitively tend to react to that person in the same way.

Whether verbally or tacitly, they agree on what's important. This shared outlook is the best guarantor that a marriage will stay on course, come hell or high water. The same is true for organizations. The best bet for success is to build relationships on shared values. Hire the right people and make them honored members of your corporate family.

While alignment is not complicated in itself and not something that requires a lot of rules and paperwork, it doesn't just happen by getting people together and issuing instructions. The foundation of alignment will always be a leader's deep and sincere concern for people. This concern is reflected in the group consciousness or spirit. It is evidenced in listening to people's concerns and ideas and a commitment to treat others as full and equal partners.

The foundation of alignment, let's be absolutely clear, is *trust.*

Trust involves recognizing that almost all people engaged in work truly want to do a good job. But they do need understanding, support, and help to guide them in their growth toward confident mastery of their operations. An effective leader will develop this potential by caring and nurturing people's skills and emotional energy.

Joe Gibbs, one of the most successful coaches in National Football League history, demonstrated his ability to bring out the best in his players through encouraging rather than berating them. When free safety Brad Edwards was new to Gibbs' Washington Redskins team, he did not play particularly well for a couple of games. However, Coach Gibbs did not tell Edwards he would be cut if he didn't play better.

"Nothing like that," Edwards said. "He came up to me in private and said, 'I know you can play better, and you need to pick it up. I know you can do better.'"

"That's all I needed to hear," Edwards said. "It totally changed my career. I wanted to do well and get better, and Coach Gibbs realized that. I didn't need to be screamed at."[4]

Corporate Culture and Social Harmony

Corporate culture and alignment are not the same, but each will reflect the other. There can be no alignment in a brutal win-lose culture that breeds animosity and back-stabbing. Alignment depends upon a spirit of cooperation and harmony. It is based on common beliefs and values. If there is to be harmony, what's right for the corporation has to be what's right for the individual. By sharing the beliefs and values of the organization, taking them to heart, people enter into a commitment to making them happen.

Daniel Goleman noted that wherever people come together to collaborate in a meeting or working on a project, they have a "group IQ," which represents the "sum total of the talents and skills of all those involved."[5] How well they accomplish their task depends on the level of that IQ.

The most important element in group intelligence, Goleman found, was not the academic intelligence level of the group's members. The key to a high group IQ is *"social harmony."* Teams that were able to create an internal harmony were able to take full advantage of their members' abilities. In groups where there was a lot of emotional and social turmoil, whether from anger or resentment or rivalries, people could not perform at their best. Harmony allows a group to take advantage of the abilities of its most creative and talented members.

Alignment Is More Than Team Building and Teamwork

Teamwork is not yet alignment, which is on a higher plateau of understanding and cooperation. But just as we often work on team building to create the proper atmosphere for entering into strategic planning, we consider team building to be a precondition for achieving alignment. This is not to say that alignment can be created in a linear training process. Alignment is not linear. It's the product of a dynamic relationship among all of the basic organizational factors. The process of building alignment is essentially a miniview of the system laid out in this book.

In alignment, everyone is brought into the Big Picture. People are able to look beyond their own roles and see how they impact on the larger process. They are encouraged to innovate and to find a better way.

We know that change is inevitable, and alignment channels change within boundaries. It holds the organization together as it evolves and invents its own future.

Synergy

When you have a group of people working together in a highly coopera-tive fashion — although there is still an allowance for conflict — you'll have *synergy*. This means that with everybody on the same track and focused on accomplishing the mission, the creative forces of the organization are un-leashed. I won't say that everything meshes like clockwork, because synergy, of necessity, allows for the expression of different views, even for arguments. With true synergy, differing views are encouraged and are significant. It is in the dynamics of conflict that new solutions are found. If you don't have dif-ferent views, you're never going to grow.

For someone's creativity to really come forth, to my mind, that person must first feel comfortable with the workplace environment. He or she must be working in the midst of a group of people where there is trust. A place where you don't say to yourself during a meeting, "Hey, I'd like to make a point or challenge what's going on here, but I don't think I'll risk it. I'm afraid somebody will shoot me down." With that kind of fear at work, you're not going to have much synergy.

Synergy helps people be themselves. When synergy is present, everyone feels a sense of inner strength and freedom. Creativity thrives in an atmo-sphere of cooperation and trust. The idea here is that one plus one equals five. As people spark thoughts in other people, creativity really takes off.

Alignment Is the Key to Spirit

With the development of true alignment comes the creation of a winning *spirit*. The two are closely interrelated. Just as alignment is unthinkable with-out teamwork, spirit is not possible without the relationship of cooperation and trust which characterize alignment.

The top person is extremely important. He or she can make or break an organization. If you have a CEO who wants to call all the shots and who can be very intimidating, you're not going to have healthy growth as a group.

In one company where we consulted, the CEO recently had been con-fronted by his executive team and told that a policy he had put together five months ago would have to change or there'd be problems. "What're you talk-ing about?" he said. "We just put a lot of effort into hammering that out, and you want to change it already?" However, when the team explained the circumstances to him, he relaxed and said he'd had no idea how various factors were evolving and that the team was right. Things would have to change.

My point here is that the team members, as a group, felt comfortable enough with the atmosphere to go to the top man and tell him his policy was off base.

A winning team is never divided against itself. It may have problems and conflicts, but it is not divided in purpose. Commonality of purpose allows team members to combine their efforts in a way that naturally creates synergy. And a way that results in that most precious attribute, *spirit.* Throughout life, in things big and small, nothing is more important than spirit.

Shortly before we flew off to provide air cover over the Normandy beaches for the D-Day landing, our group commander, Col. Red McColpin, had some final words for us. Here, as recorded in the combat history of the 404th Fighter Group, is what McColpin told us:

"...the infantry will have trouble enough landing and getting inland without being bothered by enemy aircraft. Sixteen pilots and planes, or thirty-two or forty-eight, would be a cheap price to pay to keep the beaches free....

"If your plane develops mechanical trouble, come home. If a fight develops, stay there till the last enemy plane is driven away, even if you run out of gas and have to come down in the sea... If you run out of ammunition, ram 'em...!"

Those were our orders. They came from the heart. They were spoken to pilots and crew who understood how high the stakes were for the ground forces who would hit the beaches, for the course of the war, and for the survival of all that was dear to us. That kind of spirit inspired men to accomplish the impossible.

A powerful spirit, grounded in a unity of beliefs and cooperation and trust, makes a team unstoppable.

CHAPTER

FUN AND ENJOYMENT

A merry heart doeth good like a medicine;
but a broken spirit drieth the bones.
Proverbs 17:22

Humor Is a Useful Workplace Tool

The fact that humor is good for us was known in Biblical times. Modern research has confirmed that having fun and enjoying life not only lifts our spirits, it actually benefits our health. Studies indicate that people who can "loosen up" and laugh, who allow themselves to have fun are healthier and live longer than the Eeyores of our world. Eeyore, the donkey in *Winnie-the-Pooh*, would go to any lengths to avoid being happy.

But having fun has seldom been associated with the workplace. "Work is serious," says the inner voice of the Protestant Ethic. (At least that's what the work ethic was called before political correctness.) "Fun is frivolous." "Either you work or you have fun. You don't do both."

The idea of work being fun has not been given much of a chance in the court of public opinion. It simply hasn't been tried enough to become a serious challenge to the norm. In many organizations, having and expressing a good sense of humor will typecast you as a lightweight. Teams work in deadly earnest — serious, purposeful — and miserable. People can't wait until the day ends so that they can be "human" again.

The desire to flee from unrelenting grimness is an acknowledgment that, in order to be healthy human beings we *need*, both physically and mentally, to have fun. We need fun as part of our daily living and working lives, not as an escape. Can we really spend fifty weeks a year being miserable and then be "happy" during two weeks of vacation? Would we want to?

Humor pays off. Just as it provides countless benefits to us as individuals, having fun is a useful tool in the workplace. Each of us knows that we can never do our best when we are overly tense. Our best thinking and our most productive interaction with people almost always come at a time when we are relaxed and in control of ourselves — free from the interference of mental and emotional static. The same is true for teams.

Humor and having fun in the workplace are beneficial for teamwork and human relationships, problem solving, and creativity. Having fun, enjoying what you're doing, and wanting to be there is a major part of developing *spirit*.

An Aid in Problem Solving

"Workers who have a good time are better at problem solving and are more effective on the job."

This was a finding of Dr. Alice M. Isen, a psychologist at the University of Maryland. She determined that the elation from having fun helps people recognize more complex associations and enables them to think more creatively.

Robert Ornstein, Ph.D., and David Sobel, M.D., have written a wonderful tribute to the power of joy in their book, *Healthy Pleasures*. They point out that animals, faced with a threatening situation, have two options: fight or flight. Man has a third alternative — laughter. Humor allows us to distance ourselves from trouble, making it easier to roll with life's setbacks. Laughter can free us to consider problems along more creative lines. Ornstein and Sobel found that "After viewing funny movies people tend to solve problems with more ingenuity and innovation."[1]

Relaxing Mental Tension

A growing body of research points to similar findings. Dr. David J. Abramis, a psychologist at California State University's School of Business Administration in Long Beach, found that those who have the most fun at their jobs are likely to be the most productive. He said that having fun on the job:

- Relaxes mental tension, so people can focus better on their work.
- May provide breaks from conflicts and boredom.
- Allows people to fulfill human social needs without making personal phone calls or otherwise "goofing off."

Ornstein and Sobel call healthy humor a "universal social balm" that breaks the ice, builds trust, and draws people together.

To me, *laughter is a twelfth linking skill,* a powerful tool in facilitating teamwork.

"The Pursuit of Happiness"

Abraham Lincoln said, "A man is as happy as his mind allows him to be." Regardless of the mental tapes we keep playing inside ourselves, we *can* pursue happiness, and we can make it a priority. We recall that the Declaration of Independence defines the Pursuit of Happiness as a precious birthright and one of the greatest goals of mankind.

But to bring true *joy* into our business and personal lives may require that we take a different approach from our traditional concepts of what is appropriate and inappropriate behavior.

To meet the stressful challenges of modern life, psychologist Robert J. Kriegel, with Louis Patler, has called for a new way of thinking in his book, *If it ain't broke... BREAK IT!* He says that in these rapidly changing times, our survival as thriving individuals and organizations requires that we break away from outmoded patterns into unconventional ways of thinking and doing things.[2]

Kriegel says the American obsession with "having the most toys" is so demanding that personal lives — relationships, family, and the time to enjoy them — have become impoverished. As a result, psychologists, psychiatrists, and counselors are our newest "growth industry."

Work is expected to be hard, even unpleasant, he says. The idea that it could be fun is some screwball theory cooked up in a California hot tub.

But Kriegel's interviews with top performers found that the most common ingredient for success was that *people love what they are doing.* "Doing what you love brings joy, passion, and excitement into your life. It gives you more vitality and makes you *want* to get up in the morning."

Winning is not collecting toys. It is playing the game, *"loving what you are doing and doing what you love."*

Permission to Have Fun

Incorporating humor, fun, and enjoyment into the organization's culture begins with the definition and yearly reassessment of basic *values*. Setting the stage for having fun is no isolated event. Like the development of spirit, joy evolves from the organization's foundation beliefs, its guiding principles, and its all-important *leadership*.

Giving ourselves *permission to have fun*, despite Ebeneezer Scrooge hovering in some dark corner of our working minds, is to create an atmosphere and an attitude toward life. It is a redefinition of what work is all about. It is positive, confident, and life-enhancing.

As I have said about spirit, you can pick up the "vibes" of happiness and people liking what they're doing as soon as you walk in the door of an organization. Or you can get the opposite effect — as in a suburban newspaper a close associate once visited. It was so tyrannized by the managing editor that the reporters cringed and spoke in whispers. They approached the editor like supplicants. The receptionist hardly acknowledged the visitor's presence. Her survival depended not upon doing her job with others, but upon pleasing the resident deity. It was obviously a terrible place to work. You couldn't imagine having any enjoyment in such an atmosphere.

Having Fun in Two High-Growth Companies

From their early days, we have been privileged to work with two companies, in particular, whose performance has been phenomenal and whose spirit has included a large dose of having fun. Both are high-tech, startup corporations that grew from a single person or a handful of individuals to become rising powers in their field.

Both of these companies hum. You can feel the energy around you and sense a kind of goodwill that's catching. You hear people laughing, and it's obvious that they want to be there. Ideas percolate. People are enthusiastic. Liking what they do, they're highly proficient at doing it. *The result is ever new initiatives and new solutions.*

The joyful atmosphere is no accident. It didn't just happen. Both companies have declared among their basic values that they want innovative people who can have fun and get along with others. These are the team members the companies hire and train. If someone can't catch the spirit, eventually they will not last. Neither of these two corporations merely pays lip service to their declared values. They live them.

Among the values of one of the companies is the statement, *"Politics not welcome."* We all know from our own experience that you can't be forthcoming, open, and cooperative if you're always watching your six o'clock position to keep from being jumped by bandits. Office politics is a self-serving activity that wastes energy and corrodes human relations. It is divisive rather than inclusive and is, therefore, anathema to good team spirit. Pruning it back creates space for productivity.

The first company, Strategic Technologies, Inc., stresses the human values of personal character and positive relationships, along with the ideal of excellence. In its values statement, it includes one word that is capitalized and in bold print. That concept, which stands out on the page and is meant to, is "**F-U-N**."

The second company is Zipcom, with an annual growth rate of 100 percent per year over the last three years. Its expression of values is essentially iconoclastic. The guidelines of its corporate culture don't sound at all like the traditional, straight-laced workplace in which being serious at all times is the only way to be taken seriously at any time. It stresses working with exciting people and customers in a "zany, laughter-filled environment."

Both of these companies have stated their resolve to ban office politics, insofar as possible. In word and deed, both have created an atmosphere in which people are pulling together, not apart, and are being encouraged to enjoy life. It's the kind of cooperative environment we described as being necessary for *alignment* — one in which people care and help one another. If a team excels, it is not the individual contributor, but the entire team that is rewarded.

To me, these companies have created a way of doing things that expresses a high ideal in defining the nature of work:

Truly enjoy, not merely endure.

Go to a Ball Game Together

In the summer, you see many organizations having barbecues and picnics together. Some companies make these events a regular feature of their operations. Once a year, for instance, Strategic Technologies takes the entire workforce to see the Durham Bulls play baseball. The company rents one of the special "walk around" sections at the Bulls' stadium and brings in all the refreshments that go with a baseball game: hot dogs, hamburgers, beer, soft drinks. What's interesting is that the great majority of the time is spent not on eating, drinking, or even watching the ball game, but on socializing — getting to know one another better.

A relaxed, no-pressure social setting is a different psychological place from the work environment. The issue at hand is no longer accomplishing tasks together, but having fun and enjoying each other. In this changed setting, it's easier to see people as human beings, not unlike ourselves, with personal lives and concerns much like our own.

It's important that the CEO participate. Leading the fighter squadron in Normandy, I used to wrestle or play baseball every day. On the playing field, rank meant nothing. One day I saw a new person on first base, my usual position — a stranger in a shirt with no insignia. I assumed he was someone who had flown in from the States to help us, a "tech rep" from a defense company, or Red Cross representative. After the game, I learned that the visiting first baseman was Major General Elwood R. "Pete" Quesada, the commanding general of the IXth Tactical Air Command. That was a nice trait for a commander. He was just part of the team.

The more comfortable people feel with one another, the better they're going to work together. Knowing each other better contributes to building a high level of trust. Playing ball together; exercising together; swimming together; playing touch ball, coed volleyball, badminton, or horseshoes together are all excellent ways of helping people to open up with each other. Playing together builds cooperation, harmony, and spirit. It leads to a higher degree of creativity.

The Gift of Humor

In any area of our lives, humor is important to our own well-being and to our ability to influence and work with others. This is true in business, in government, and in our families and personal life.

Nothing breaks the tension in a family dispute like being able to laugh at yourself. The next time you're locking horns with your spouse or your children, with both of you righteously convinced that your position is unassailable, let things rest for a minute and then toss in a quip that shows you realize you're being a little bit silly. Suddenly the situation doesn't seem so serious any more. You find that maybe it isn't *all that* important. There's nothing like a little laughter for regaining your perspective.

Leaders in all walks of life have found that a humorous touch acts as a

bridge between them and those they wish to influence. It also can help political and other leaders deal with difficult issues. Humor adds the emotional
element of *feeling*.

One of the most beloved Americans of the twentieth century was Will
Rogers, whose wise and incisive commentary on American politics helped the
country endure the Great Depression. On his radio show, he would use the
daily newspaper as the source of his humor, since to him, nothing was so
funny as the truth. He once quipped, "I'm not a member of any organized
political party. I'm a Democrat."

Franklin Roosevelt bore some of the heaviest burdens of any American
president, from the Depression into the global conflict of World War II. His
wit, like that of Winston Churchill, was a great asset in dealing with friend
and foe alike. Once when he had been bitterly accused of sending a naval ship
back to the Aleutians to pick up his famous dog, Fala, Roosevelt broadcast a
mock defense to the nation. He said that while *he* didn't take personal offense at
these attacks, and his wife, Eleanor, didn't take personal offense, Fala *did!* Whatever the truth was, in that instant he took the wind out of his opponents' sails.

A great part of John Kennedy's appeal was in his style. The good looks,
grace, and the soaring ideas were accompanied by a quick wit and an impish
grin. His press conferences were *fun*. He was endearing in relaxed moments,
such as in the home movie in which he told his small son, "Uh, John-John, I
don't think you should call the president of the United States an old poop."
His relaxed manner and humor devastated Richard Nixon in the well-known
presidential debates.

The same was true for Ronald Reagan. Reagan's optimism helped the
country to regain its pride and put the agony of Vietnam behind it. His quips,
after an assassination attempt, that he "forgot to duck" and he hoped "the
surgeons are Republicans" were reassuring to Americans. His affability and
sense of well-being helped create a bond of understanding with Soviet Pre-
mier Mikhail Gorbachev, as the "evil empire" collapsed. Reagan's warm personality overwhelmed Jimmy Carter, who seemed stiff in comparison.

I remember watching television and seeing Bill Clinton absolutely crack
up during some tense negotiations with Russian President Boris Yeltsin over
the question of NATO expansion. I believe that the rapport between these
two men, who were able to laugh together, eased their difficult tasks.

No American leader is better remembered for the gift of humor than

Abraham Lincoln. In the dark early years of the Civil War, Lincoln was be-deviled by opposition from his Army commander, George B. McClellan. McClellan, who liked to be thought of as "the Young Napoleon," built a fine new Army but was reluctant to fight with it. Unable to get McClellan to move, Lincoln said, "If McClellan is not using the Army, I should like to borrow it for a while."

Humor aided Lincoln in dealing with McClellan's insolence. Without winning any battles, the general kept demanding more guns, men, and horses, and at the same time, telling Lincoln how to run the country. Lincoln said it reminded him of the Irishman whose horse kicked up and got his foot caught in the stirrup. "If you're going to get on," the Irishman said, "I'm going to get off."

Angry at Lincoln's requests for more detailed reports, McClellan sent him a dispatch that said, "We have just captured six cows. What shall we do with them?" Lincoln wired back, "As to the six cows captured — milk them."

Humor was Lincoln's greatest ally in bearing the burdens of the war. A week after the indecisive battle of Antietam, the bloodiest day in the history of American arms, Lincoln called his War Cabinet together. The mood was grim, but the President insisted on reading aloud to them a piece from a popular humorist of the time, Artemus Ward. When he was finished, Lincoln laughed heartily, but not a single member of the Cabinet laughed with him.

With a long sigh, Lincoln said, "Gentlemen, why don't you laugh? With the fearful strain that is upon me night and day, if I did not laugh I should die, and you need this medicine as much as I do."

And then he told them the reason he had called them together and sol-emnly read to them a document he had decided to issue. It was the Emanci-pation Proclamation.

Bend Like a Pine Tree

One of our greatest enemies in life is taking ourselves too seriously. If we think we're too dignified to get down in the mud when we have to, or too important to carry out tasks that are "beneath" us, or that we can't compro-mise because we've got a monopoly on being right — we're setting ourselves up for a fall.

We can't always laugh at ourselves when we'd like to, but what if we could? What if, the next time you're provoked, instead of getting tight in the throat and having the adrenaline start to pump, you just relax and laugh it off? The only power people have over you is the power you give them. So you smile and calmly disarm your opponent with grace and charm. When you have control over your own emotions, you have authority. Being able to laugh and not take yourself too seriously gives you that control.

Learn to bend with the inevitable, like a pine tree. When a load of ice coats the pine tree's branches, it will bend lower and lower as the weight accumulates. But being flexible, it will not break. A fruit tree, however, stands straight and rigid, and when the ice load becomes too heavy, its branches snap.

Humor is a key to maintaining our flexibility. And while determination and perseverance are virtues, pressing on against the inevitable is courting defeat. You might have the right direction but be a little off course, or you may think something's perfect for you and find it isn't at all. Sometimes you have to be flexible, reassess, and start out again. You don't have to compromise your principles, but you have to look at the situation in a spirit of give and take.

There is a well-known prayer that originated in eighteenth century Germany, although it is usually attributed to Reinhold Niebuhr. To me the words are a meaningful expression of the need to maintain flexibility and perspective and bend with the inevitable:

> *God, grant me the serenity to accept those things I cannot change,*
> *the courage to change those I can,*
> *and the wisdom to know the difference.*

CHAPTER

LEADERSHIP

Never compromise your personal integrity. Be willing to examine decisions
with a set of critical values that remain true to your beliefs.
Donald E. Petersen

Leadership: A Summing Up

Leadership is not something separate from the fundamentals of building a great organization. Since it is integral to every principle and every step along the way, you have been absorbing elements of leadership throughout the book. In fact, leadership is a summing up of all the preceding chapters.

Nothing happens to pursue a goal without leadership of some kind. Leadership is the prime source, like the hand of God, that sets everything in motion. The leader's role never ends. It influences every stage of operations.

Since a leader is defined as one who leads others or has followers, leadership is essentially a *relationship* business. The leader establishes the nature of the playing field and sets organizational standards, from hiring the right people to defining values and helping to determine the objectives and how they will be achieved.

All of this, step by step, is created from the *vision* of leaders, whatever their position or level within the organization. Vision is a grand view of where you want to go, but for it to have wings, it also will inspire others to go there and show them the way. All the way through the process of building an organization and guiding it to greatness, the leader provides the way.

Because the influence of leadership is so great, from inception to product or service, the organization and its relative level of success will always reflect the personality and character of its leaders.

Concern for People

While the World War II generation was characterized by a top-down, command management style, I found that pure authoritarianism wasn't the best answer then, and it certainly isn't today. The best leaders in the war were those who not only commanded their men, but who also cared for them, inspired them, and made them want to follow.

The core value that made everything work was *belief and trust in people*.

A classic example was General George Patton's relief of the 101st Airborne at Bastogne during the Battle of the Bulge. Fully involved in combat, the Third Army somehow disengaged, changed its direction of advance, and raced hundreds of miles, day and night, to go directly into battle. It was one of the greatest feats of American military history. Patton's men didn't love him, but he made them feel proud of themselves — and that pride translated into fighting spirit.

Dwight Eisenhower was a different and perhaps more modern kind of leader. Always conscious of the Big Picture, he had a genius for getting along with people and winning their cooperation. It took the patience of Job to weather Field Marshal Bernard Montgomery's ego and to fend off Winston Churchill's brilliant ideas, which kept springing up like marsh grass. Besides being thorough and determined, Eisenhower was master of the human element.

Leadership, based on core values that include a genuine *concern for people*, is the indispensable element of building a great organization.

Character and Earning Trust

INTEGRITY: THE CURRENCY BY WHICH PEOPLE JUDGE YOU

To be a great leader you have to have great followers. To want to follow, we have to believe in and *trust* someone who is worthy of our respect. Leadership is essentially a matter of *character*, and to me, the basis of character is *integrity*. Without integrity, there can be no real trust and no depth of relationship, in business or personal life.

Your character is the currency by which people judge you. I was president of an accident board in the Philippines after World War II which had the task of investigating flying accidents. One pilot landed his plane on its belly, which meant that for whatever reason, he didn't have the landing gear down. When he came before the board, he saluted and offered no excuses. "Sir," he said, "I goofed. I just forgot it." The board took five minutes to deliberate his case and gave him a positive rating.

Another flyer in another time and place was headed for an unintended belly landing until a last-minute flare from the ground control sent him around for another approach. While he was in the landing pattern, this time with his gear down, he came up on the radio. "I've had it with this equipment failure!," he said. "I want the engineering officer, the line chief, the chief inspector, the flight chief, and the crew chief to meet me on the tarmac!" That pilot insisted that his gear wouldn't come down. But I knew the P-47 like the back of my hand. You put the handle down and the gear goes down, with or without hydraulic pressure.

The same accident had happened to both people, but the way they reacted to it said everything about who they were. The first pilot had been honest. He could hold his head high and feel good about himself. The second flyer showed that he was not someone you could trust. In gaining trust, nothing is more important than maintaining absolute honesty and integrity.

STEADINESS, FAIRNESS, AND "CONSTANCY"

Former Cabinet Member John W. Gardner wrote that one of two prerequisites for trust in a leader is *steadiness*.[1] An unpredictable leader drives the followers nuts. The other prerequisite is *fairness*. This applies both when issues are being decided out in the open, and in the back room, where people seek privileged access.

In his classic study of leadership, *Why Leaders Can't Lead*, Warren Bennis lists these skills among the four principle "Leadership Competencies": management of *trust* and management of *self*. He says that the main determinant of trust is reliability, or what he calls *"constancy."* When a leader is reliable, "Whether you like it or not, you always know where he's coming from, what he stands for." Managing the self is knowing your skills and deploying them effectively.[2]

CARING

Character has a lot to do with *caring* about others, and it is a necessary quality for entering into a lasting commitment of any kind. It's the hallmark of a good husband or wife or parent, just as it is the prime quality of a true leader in business or church or the community. Character is the basis of good citizenship.

But character in any of us and in an organization can be negative as well as positive, or anywhere in between. The culture of the home or the work-place flows from character, like water from a well. The spirit that flows with it will be equally positive, negative, or neutral.

THE INNER YOU

It's not what we wish or hope that molds our character and personality. It's the way we think. The kind of message we direct inwardly dictates the kind of experience we are going to have with life.

The bottom line is what we *expect*. Expect to put your best foot forward and you will. Expect to lose — that you're in over your head — and be as-sured you will be. Think a task extremely difficult, or think you'll have fun doing it, and either way that's the experience you'll have. Hopes, wishes, and aspirations start the process working, but until you take the message inside and turn dreams into *expectations*, they will not happen.

Denis Waitley, one of the world's top social scientists, stated, "After over 20 years of research into the field of high level human achievement, I am convinced that we literally talk ourselves into and out of every victory or defeat in the game of life."

At the heart of sustained morale and motivation, John Gardner saw two ele-ments that appear somewhat contradictory. The first is a positive attitude toward the future and toward what we can accomplish, and the other was *"recognition that life is not easy and that nothing is ever finally safe."* [3]

"KNOW THYSELF"

It's no accident of history that the words of Socrates, "Know thyself," are still honored in our culture after more than two thousand years. Relationships with other people begin in the relationship with ourselves. You can't be one thing to yourself and something else to the world. Somewhere there's a disconnect.

Since any organization reflects the values and vision of the leader, the leader must look into his own heart for what the organization will be. As Viktor Frankl said, man's primary goal in life is a search for meaning, the meaning that only he can find, in his own way.[4] The leader has to stand on solid ground, knowing his own capabilities and those of others, to delegate effectively, to inspire, and to lead.

BE SQUARE WITH YOURSELF

We can always play someone else's game, but for us to be truly effective as leaders or followers, our efforts in the external world must be in harmony with our deepest inner beliefs and our essential identity. Only then are we living in our own integrity. Mike Vance has said, "How people handle their personal lives always comes out in business."[5] Both halves have to be in consonance. If you can't trust a person in one aspect of their lives, you can't trust them in another.

It takes courage to go it alone and to do what is right for you, regardless of what is expected. Mahatma Gandhi, whose strategy of passive resistance won independence for the Indian subcontinent, was one of the greatest moral and political leaders of the twentieth century. Gandhi, who lived this message, declared:

All is well with you even though everything seems to go dead wrong,
if you are square with yourself. Conversely, all is not well with you although
everything outwardly may seem to go right, if you are not square with yourself.

Exemplary Leadership

Leaders are people who can see beyond the horizon, who share with us a dream and lift our spirits and make us believe that we can reach the dream. In their recent book, *The Leadership Challenge*, James Kouzes and Barry Posner published the results of a study they had done on what it takes to become a leader.[6] An analysis of thousands of cases revealed that the exemplary leaders followed five fundamental practices:

- *Leaders challenge the process.*
  They look for opportunities to change the status quo and for ways to improve the organization, and they experiment and take risks.
- *Leaders inspire a shared vision.*
  They believe they can make a difference. They envision the future, and through their strong appeal, enlist others in the dream.
- *Leaders enable others to act.*
  They foster collaboration and build spirited teams with mutual

respect and an atmosphere of trust and human dignity. They share information and "give their own power away" so that others may be empowered.

- *Leaders model the way.*
  They create standards of excellence and set the example for others, and they establish values about how people should be treated.
- *Leaders encourage the heart.*
  To keep hope and determination alive, leaders recognize the contributions individuals make and celebrate accomplishments to make everyone "feel like a hero."

Kouzes and Posner stress that positive leadership can be learned — through belief in yourself, trial and error, observing others, and lifelong education and training. They point out that "The mastery of the art of leadership comes with the mastery of the self." Leadership development is self-development.[7] As I have said, it begins with character.

Leaders, Managers, and Bosses

Leaders and managers have different roles, although either can switch roles or play both roles at the same time. Nonetheless, there is a clear distinction between the two. Warren Bennis has said that "Leaders are people who do the right thing; managers are people who do things right."[8]

THE LEADER

Leadership always comes first, providing the vision, the inspiration, and the strategy for the long term. The leader is the architect who creates the grand design. Leadership focuses on the Big Picture and is process — and value — oriented. Since leaders are defined by their relationship with their followers, true leaders must have the ability to inspire others to pursue their dream. A leader has to be willing to lead and have the courage to put himself on the line.

Leadership is a *pull* rather than a *push* operation. No one can be coerced to do his best. But even when a crisis arises and the leader has to call the shots — direct, control, and drive to get the job done — the team will come through. The true leader has established a relationship of mutual trust with the team members, and they accept responsibility for accomplishing the task. They're good because they want to be.

THE HEART OF LEADERSHIP

Over many years of command and business consulting, I have observed many leaders, and I have found that those who were truly outstanding shared some basic traits. To me, these are the heart of leadership.

As a colonel stationed in England, I found these qualities exemplified in a junior captain I enjoyed flying with, barreling at low level across the lush English countryside in our F-100 Super Sabres. He was an outstanding flyer and a natural leader. The characteristics I saw in him are those I have observed in other true leaders.

- *Vision*
- *Deep inner core values*
- *A deep and sincere concern for people*
- *The will to be a strong team player*
- *The ability to encourage and inspire others*

The young captain was always looking ahead and knew where he wanted to go and where the organization should be going toward continual improvement. He had an ability to get along with people at all levels, and he had the special kind of personality that generates *esprit de corps*. The captain, Merrill A. McPeak, rose to general and chief of staff, the highest position in the U.S. Air Force.

THE MANAGER

Management is the operation that gets the job done. An effective manager also has to have an astute awareness of the long-term goal and the vision that underlies the mission. Management then provides the short-term, precise, and bottom-line focus. This is the product-oriented and tactical area.

But even on a day-to-day basis, managers are often leaders. Some qualify and some don't. Leaders create followers. Those managers who use the "park your brains outside and do what I tell you" approach have neither followers nor true power.

A good manager is clear in his or her goal and can delegate, direct, and control, establishing a plan with a timetable on who does what. Bad management is to tell people how to do the job and insist they do it your way. Tell them what you want done and leave the "how-to" up to them.

THE BOSS

The boss style of management is the pure "push" operation. Bossism is not leadership. This is the hard-nosed driver, the dictator, the autocrat — who is now supposed to have disappeared like the dinosaurs. *But wait. Isn't that a tyrannosaurus rex over there in that office?* The boss stifles the human spirit, and along with it, the organization's innovation and creativity. People do what they are told to do and nothing more. The boss can get results but not dedication.

POETIC JUSTICE

When I was a first lieutenant at a training base in Tallahassee, Florida, we were flying the P-39 Airacobra fighter. It had two toggle switches on the dash, one for the flaps and one for the landing gear, and it was easy to get the two confused. Hitting the wrong one, raising the flaps or gear at the wrong time, could be disastrous.

One day a full colonel came flying in, parked his P-39, and gathered all the pilots together in the base theater. He began prancing back and forth. Then he erupted. He was a classic "boss."

"We in headquarters have had enough of these stupid accidents!" he shouted. "I've never seen such dumb flying in my life. You guys are a bunch of dummies! You people are such imbeciles that you can't keep your head straight on which switch to push! If you can't start thinking, we'll by God let you go, and find somebody who can!"

Finally, he stormed out into the Florida sunshine, got into his P-39, taxied down the runway, gathered speed — and dropped his plane on its belly.

The Leadership Triangle

Leadership pulls together the inner core of an organization. It is the fourth

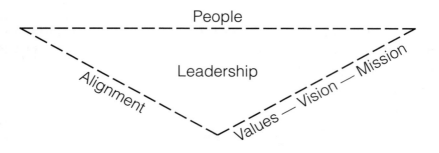

The Leadership Triangle

element that binds together the core elements of *People, Values,* and *Alignment.* Leadership is the seen or unseen hand in all things, the guiding and unifying force.

The pyramid is inverted to indicate that *People* are at the top. Reversing the traditional management structure acknowledges that people are the organization's greatest resource. Notice that the triangle is flat. Its compression means that you do not have a multi-tiered managerial hierarchy.

The dashed lines show that it is an *open system* in which people continue to think both internally and externally. Solid lines would convey a closed-off, independent system. With system openness, the organization emphasizes communication and relationship, from team to team and department to department, and in checking the pulse of things going on in the outside world. The system is also open to new ideas and new and better ways of getting the job done.

Leadership is what makes it work.

Applying Different Leadership Styles

A leader has to be flexible and apply different styles of leadership, depending upon the needs of the situation. There is a time for directing and driving and a time for coaching and supporting. You change leadership style, because the situation changes. An emergency comes up, or someone has been performing well but his or her performance has dropped off. You need to deal with that individual on the appropriate level. You may have to drop back from coaching and encouraging to directing.

One of the greatest challenges in applying the right style of leadership is in developing your people — so that they can reach and sustain a high level of performance. The kind of guidance you provide has to meet the needs of the individual *at that time.* At the beginning, for example, you want to lay out precisely what you want done, and as the person gains competence and confidence, you can back off and shift to a supporting and coaching mode.

Situational Leadership

Ken Blanchard calls this process "Situational Leadership" and has developed a highly regarded model for applying leadership on a flexible basis.[9] The system, called SLII, is based on a relationship between the individual's development level and the kind of leadership style the leader provides.

Blanchard's SLII Model

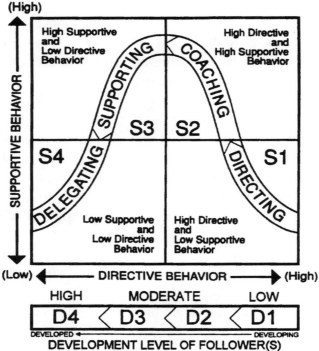

Courtesy Ken Blanchard

Each of four leadership styles, *Directing, Coaching, Supporting* and *Delegating,* comes into play during the successive stages of an employee's development. A leader begins with directing — telling and showing people what to do and providing close, personal supervision. As the individual's skills and confidence grow, the leadership style becomes more supportive until, in the final stage, the leader can let go and turn over responsibility to the individual.

Many leaders and managers have been automatically applying this method for years, but sometimes they get stuck in either control or support and lose sight of the individual's development. The person is then stuck with being under- or over-managed.

Skills and capabilities are not global. A person may be a D4 (the highest level of development), for example, in sales. But when you ask him "To whip up a budget," the outstanding salesperson is not a D4 anymore. Your goal is to move people into the D4 level of skills and confidence for specific task areas so that you, the leader, can apply your skills where they're most needed.

SHOW, WATCH, ENCOURAGE, SOLO

This flexible style of leadership is essentially the approach I learned as commandant of major flying schools in the Air Force. In 1951, I was the training group commander for three schools in Valdosta, Georgia: instrument instructor pilots' school, a school for the transition from prop to jet aircraft, and a third school for teaching the jet pilots all-weather operations.

We would give the student an overview of the program, like an orientation in a new company. We began the flying phase by *telling* the student what to do, then *showing* him what to do. The student would perform the maneuver for the instructor pilot (IP), who would *observe* and provide a "well done" or an analysis of what had gone wrong. We'd repeat the cycle until it was correct. Finally the pilot would solo and practice ever more difficult tasks until they became second nature. Along the way our job was to *encourage* the student and build his *confidence.*

To encourage creativity, we never insisted that every pilot perform every maneuver exactly like his IP. The end result had to be correct, but he could do it in his own way.

This is the simple, common-sense approach that many of us learned in our families. Just as I had chores to do when I was growing up, each of my four sons had regular tasks to perform. I'd go through the cycle of showing them what to do, watching, and then finally being able to back off, but it was sometimes difficult. I'd get frustrated and want to get in and do the job myself because I could do it so much better and faster. But letting them learn to do it themselves paid off dividends in the long term. Developing people is a long-term business.

Effective Delegating

One of the trickiest leadership talents to develop is good delegation. First you have to understand the dimensions of the project to be delegated, and then you have to match up the requirements with the right person or persons. You can't just grab somebody from the ranks and say, "Now you are responsible for this piece of work" — if the person is neither suited for the task nor interested in it. This is a recipe for failure, and the failure rests squarely on the shoulders of the person doing the delegating.

You make delegation a two-way street by first establishing a basis of understanding with likely candidates. Talk through the parameters of the task or ongoing responsibility as thoroughly as you can, seeking their input and feedback. What do they think about taking on the job? Although they may be a little reluctant to level with you, do your best to figure out where they're coming from. See if anything about the task gets their juices flowing. Delegation by negotiation is one of the linking skills in team building.

Once you have identified a suitable candidate and the person is at least *reasonably* interested, the next step is to provide any training that may be necessary. Typically, during the training process, the person's confidence will rise and fall as the individual struggles to achieve the kind of mastery that will be needed long-term if the company is to get quality results.

Like teaching a child to ride a bicycle, the important thing is knowing when to hold onto the handlebars and when to let go. You also have to set some standards for tolerable mistakes, and both you and the person to whom you are delegating must have *the same notion* as to what those standards are.

This is a sensitive issue. Too many leaders hold back on delegating to people who have real talent out of fear that the person will shine too brightly and attract more attention from higher management than they get. Here we need to take our cue from such great coaches as Bear Bryant of Alabama, in football, and Rick Pitino of the University of Kentucky and the Boston Celtics in basketball. Both of these coaches fearlessly trained great assistants who went on to take head coaching jobs where they would compete with their mentors. Both encouraged their assistants to reach for the stars, even if they would be future opponents.

"Be the best you can," these two superb coaches were saying. "I'll deal with the consequences of your greatness. The last thing I want to do is to hold you back."

In corporate America, the great organizations have the same spirit.

Get Out of the Way and Let It Happen

Harry Truman once said, "It's amazing what you can accomplish if you don't give a damn who gets the credit."

What we call "ego" can be a positive or negative force, giving us a secure concept of ourselves and providing drive and self-confidence — or blocking our vision of reality and demanding that we control everything around us. The need to control and dominate is just that: a need. What appears to be an inflated ego in someone who has to maintain complete control may in actuality be a deep insecurity. The person is threatened by anything he or she cannot dominate.

The pure win-lose approach, applied in all situations with all people at all times is not leadership. Neither is it friendship. Letting go takes trust in yourself.

Having brought the person along until he has achieved a high level of competence and confidence in his ability, you can now *get out of the way and let it happen.* After you have turned over responsibility, your task is to provide guidance, support, and coaching wherever necessary. Check up, be there on an on-call basis, but get out of the way. The goal for a leader is to be needed as little as possible.

The Leadership Cycle

The Leadership Cycle provides a guide for getting an organization going, monitoring its progress, and trouble shooting. It says, "Here are the bases you've got to touch." You can walk through the action steps sequentially to see where you are at any time and identify areas that need attention. You might take a hard look at Phase III, Empowerment, and find that people have been insufficiently trained or over-supervised. If that's correct, you can go back a step and see if your strategy's outdated. Or maybe the mission is fuzzy. The cycle helps you pinpoint problems and what needs to be done.

The Leadership Cycle

I. CLARIFYING MISSION: Ensure that your mission expresses true core values and that individuals at every level have a hand in preparing it, that it tells why you exist, is challenging, attainable, and inspiring.

II. STRATEGIC PLANNING AND DECISION MAKING: Strategic planning establishes a precise focus, with goals and action steps that say who does what and when.

III. EMPOWERING YOURSELF AND OTHERS: This is the result of the development process that leads to self-confidence and mutual trust, which makes effective delegation possible.

IV. MEASUREMENT AND FEEDBACK: Seek regular feedback through reports, talking to your people, clients, and customers. Ask, "How are we doing?" "How can we serve you better?" "What do you see as several of your most pressing problems down the road ahead?"

V. ADJUSTING AND IMPROVING: Make adjustments based on measurement and feedback. You are always looking for ways to improve.

VI. REWARDING: Reward provides positive feedback, which is the most effective form of motivating. There's nothing like telling your staff that you'll all be having a day at the beach and it's on the company.

Throughout the cycle, the focus remains on *people* — their development, encouragement, and support. Aggressively seek feedback and be prepared to listen. When you find a lack of dedication and initiative, *take a hard look at how people are being treated at all levels.*

Men and Women — Different Leadership Styles

The fact that women are different from men doesn't come as much of a surprise to any of us, but just how do they differ as leaders and managers? What is the effect of females as they attain ever greater presence and prominence in the workplace? My wife, Marilyn, has contributed the following thoughts.

Women are taught to be relational and men are more often taught to be competitive and task-oriented. Women tend to bring their own approach to the world of leadership and management. Being generally more feeling (than thinking) oriented than men, they place greater emphasis on people values and are more sensitive to what others are experiencing.

Male or female, you will probably not find this to be universally true in your own experience. Everyone is an individual, and female success has long been shaped by the need to compete with men, even to overcompensate for their femininity.

But the natural female operating style is less confrontational, and women are more likely to seek consensus through negotiation than to go for the win-lose showdown. In fact, the style that comes naturally to women fits perfectly with today's changing concepts of leadership — away from the command and control pyramid toward coaching, supporting, and encouraging. Women can be great nurturers. They tend to listen and communicate better, which leads to a higher level of cooperation.

Male leaders and managers need to recognize that women are different emotionally and culturally. They are by nature more empathetic and can be more expressive and, at the same time, more vulnerable. They are likely to seek consensus in decision making and to be less aggressive. Both of these traits can be positive and should not be seen as weaknesses. Women are much more open than men and need a two-way street in their work relationship.

Leadership of the future will have to be *cooperative* rather than coercive, because nothing else will work in a highly complex, interrelated, and techno-logical environment. We need to recognize the unique characteristics of women and let them play to their strong suit. We're all going in the same direction.

CHAPTER

EXECUTION:
THE ART & SCIENCE
OF MAKING IT HAPPEN

A great strategy poorly executed will absolutely fail.
A mediocre strategy flawlessly executed will win.
Mike Shook
President, Strategic Technologies, Inc.

The Payoff

It was a real kick to shove the throttle forward and, with a mighty roar of the 2,000 hp engine, feel the P-47 pick up speed, roll fast along the steel plank runway, and then lift off and soar above the green fields of England or Normandy.

The mission was under way. The strategic and tactical planning was done. The frag order had come down in the middle of the night, and the pilots had been briefed at daybreak. The armorers had been busy hanging 500-lb. fragmentation bombs on the shackles under our wings, and the engineering and communications crews had completed their final checks. Everything came down to this moment — the point of *execution*.

This is the point at which your values, vision, mission, strategy, and goals come to bear. This is the payoff. To execute your mission is to carry out, on a daily basis, those tasks for which your organization exists.

No Finish Line

Execution is carrying out a strategy, but it is much, much more than that. A combat mission was a single point in time, but in a larger sense, just as leadership cannot be separated from the entire cycle of operations, everything that goes into accomplishing the mission represents execution. To simplify, we talk about execution as if it were a separate step, isolated, distinct from day-to-day operations. It isn't. It *is* day-to-day operations. It's how you do everything at all times. Execution reflects not only your competence; it is also the manifestation of your leadership, corporate culture, and spirit.

As Robert Parrott, Zipcom marketing director, has said, "Execution is performing the task day to day. It's not bound in time to *after*. You can't say 'I'm executing now.' There's no finish line. You're applying goals all the way along."

When an athlete performs a pole vault, running up to the point of takeoff is preparation for the jump, but there is no distinct point at which the execution begins. Are you executing when you start the run? Or when you put the pole in the ground? Or when you're airborne, sailing over the bar? It's a continuous motion, the way you complete a cycle.

It's All a Function of Execution

The CEO of one of the most successful young software companies in the Southeast, Mike Shook, says *"Business is just purely execution."*

He told the story of having addressed an industry forum of some 150 presidents of companies similar to his and explaining his company's business model, its method of doing business, its focus and tactics, and its means of doing customer definition. At the end of the meeting, one of the CEOs stood up and said, "I am absolutely shocked that you, as the president of a company, would stand up here in front of your competitors and tell them what your strategies are."

"My comment was simple," Shook said. "There's not one thing that I talked about that's not absolute Business 101. *The game is execution. I'm betting that I can out-execute our competition.*"

"What are we doing that's rocket science? It's very, very simple," he said. Success is in "bear-hugging the customer with value" and "trying to make money at what you're doing." Shook's formula is to develop sound strategies, "really execute," and determine the appropriate metrics to measure whether the company is winning or losing. With a precisely defined and expanding customer base, Shook and his people try out a new proposition, and if their metrics say it doesn't work, they alter the strategy. "But it's all a function of execution," he said. "It's really a linear thing that you have to do."

Shook's company, Strategic Technologies, Inc., has established a successful pattern of internal processes, including how they qualify their customers, which is "just how we play the game." "You have a guarantee of success if you do these things," he said. "You can't *not* do these things. If someone in the company wants to go their own way, it breaks the pattern of execution. And execution is the methodology."

Shook hypothesized an example of opening a branch office in another city in the Southeast, where the branch manager would say to him, "This market's a little different from the market in Raleigh. We want to execute another strategy." Shook's response would be this: "Our entire infrastructure is built around supporting *our* strategy. So even if yours is better, you can't pull it off, because there's no one to execute it for you." But in executing the company's strategy, the branch manager could do it in any way that would feel comfortable for him.

Shook says he still believes in the "*linear approach to doing business.*" You do this, then this, then this. You check the metrics and ask, "Is it good?" "Do you retool? Do you reengineer? Do you press on? Do you back off?" It's all a tactical call, he says. And it's all execution.

> *How many football games have been won by someone throwing the Hail Mary pass? When the Dallas Cowboys come to town, you've got reels and reels of film that say exactly, precisely what they're going to do. Their running back, Emmett Smith, is going to run the ball thirty times a game, and Dallas is saying, "Stop me!" And that's what business is: "Stop me."*
>
> **Mike Shook**

The Art and Science

Execution is the art and science of making it happen.

The art is the *leadership* side. Art is the emotional, creative, designing sphere that has to do with people and relationships. It encompasses values and vision. Art is in the emotional intelligence of self-mastery, responding appropriately to the situation, and it is in bringing people together and influencing and inspiring them to attain a goal. Art is in problem solving as well as in creating teamwork. Ultimately, the art of execution is evidenced in the corporate culture and spirit.

The science side, represented by the outer circle in the hub and wheel diagram below, answers the logically quantifiable questions, "Who, what, when, how, where, why?" It has some semblance of mathematical logic. These are the "how-to" tools of management. This is where the goals get transformed into time-phased, measurable, and accountable action.

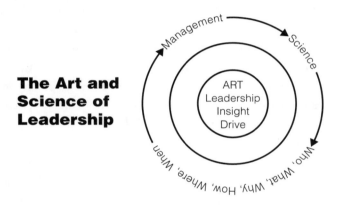

The Art and Science of Leadership

Both the art and the science are indispensable. In our work we have found that if you have both — a good organization with strong leadership — we can accomplish programs in two or three hours that would take a day to accomplish where the leadership is mediocre. A solid leader is going to pick up the ball and run with it, like Donald Petersen, former Ford CEO and chairman. His commitment to quality resulted in the Taurus, which pushed Honda aside to become the best-selling car in America. The art of execution is in leadership, follow-up, and with Mies van der Rohe's architectural principle, "Less is more." This means to simplify your management style, grow, support, and encourage your people and let them make things happen.

Pulling It All Together

Making it happen depends upon the actions of leadership and people, and each has separate tasks to perform. A key to great execution is to be always trying to find a way of doing things better. Execution goes hand in hand with the restless quest for continuing improvement.

The flow chart below is the same as the one you saw in chapter three, "Planning," with the addition of the specific "Execution" phase. It traces the steps of the organization-building process, from the definition of values, vision, and mission through goal-setting to short-term tactical planning to execution.

The Art and Science of Execution

Mission Values Vision People Alignment Leadership					
Corporate How can we do better? • Challenges • Opportunities • Ideas • Needs • Prioritize	**Corporate** • Values • Mission • Strategy • Goals	**Departments Teams Projects** How can we do better? • Success factors • Major strength to reinforce • Major weakness to overcome • Programs to discontinue • Prioritize	**Department** • Values • Mission • Goals	**Action Plans** • Specific • Time phase • Measurable • Options • Accountability	**Organizational Actions** • Make plans happen • Measure–Analyze–Coach • Organizational growth & development • Major weakness to overcome • Programs to discontinue • Prioritize **Everyone's Actions** • Continuing improvement at all levels • Work together • Measure • Breakthroughs • Action **Individual Actions** • Develop and blend individual and organizational values — mission — goals • Make full use of organization improvement opportunities/ program • Amplify as needed for personal and professional growth and development

Planning

Strategic   **Tactical**   **Execution**

The blocks on the right indicate actions that the organization and the individuals need to undertake on a regular basis. These are specific operational actions to be carried out by the three action levels on the chart (organization's, everyone's, the individual's).

Remember that treating execution as a separate phase is merely a shorthand means of focusing on what has to be done after the strategic and tactical planning have been completed. In reality, everything is ongoing and everything is execution.

ORGANIZATIONAL ACTIONS
- *Make plans happen.*
- *Measure — analyze — coach.*
- *Plan organizational growth and development.*
- *Note major weaknesses to overcome.*
- *Determine programs to discontinue.*
- *Prioritize.*
- *Attend to return on investment always.*
- *Reward creativity, breakthroughs, exceptional performance.*

EVERYONE'S ACTIONS
- *Pursue continuing improvement at all levels.*
- *Work together.*
- *Measure.*
- *Target breakthroughs.*
- *Take action — make it happen.*

INDIVIDUAL ACTIONS
- *Develop and blend individual and organizational values, mission, and goals.*
- *Make full use of organization's improvement opportunities and programs.*
- *Amplify as needed for personal and professional growth and development.*

System Openness

One of the characteristics of a great organization is a free flow of information and ideas that promotes continuous improvement through innovation. Recall that the triangle of people, values, and alignment is an open system. This is the environment of listening and communicating, the two most important of the eleven linking skills.

An open system indicates a "vision field," which releases the synergy of human relationships and encourages creativity. Openness is an attitude of actively seeking and sharing information, reaching out, being receptive to and encouraging new ideas. In a closed system, information is hoarded and compartmentalized.

In this environment of free-flowing communications, people are encouraged to look beyond their own immediate concerns and to be aware of individuals and teams that in any way impact on them. Everyone should know what happens before the action or product gets to them, what happens after it leaves them, and what the end result is. End-result orientation widens an individual's vision and helps to make that person an owner of the mission.

Organize Feedback

All organizations are systems, with every element affecting every other, and all systems provide some form of feedback. An example of feedback, provided by business consultant Ron Guzik, is adjusting the water in your shower.[1] You're standing under the water, and if it's too hot you turn it down. But then it's too cold, so you jump in and out of the water, turning it up and down, more moderately, until you've got it right.

In business, we may swing erratically between doing no advertising at all, for example, and then spend more than we should on a short campaign. When the campaign brings unsatisfactory results, we shut down the advertising again. What we really needed was perhaps a steady, moderately-budgeted campaign.

Adjusting our systems in response to either positive or negative feedback from the market may take weeks to months or years. The ideal is to wait until you are sure about a trend and then act decisively.

You can seek feedback in many ways, including Tom Peters' MBWA (Management By Walking Around) and climate surveys, which question people on their feelings about the organization. Typical questions are, "Is it a good place to work?" "Does it encourage growth?" "Do people work well with one another?"

Ron Guzik writes that "Smart companies organize feedback."[2] Airlines and motels provide short questionnaires for their customers to rate their service, and publications print readership surveys. Good managers spend a lot of time listening to their field representatives. Whatever the size of your organization, you should contact the people with whom you do business to ask them key questions on a regular, planned basis. Organize getting the feedback you need and act on it as soon as the picture is clear.

Checklist for Success

You can use a simple check chart to take a systems look at how decisions are made in your organization and who is responsible for what. The chart was developed by Al Stark, former vice president of human resources, Rubbermaid Corporation. *The Check Chart for Management Action* shows the extent to which decision-making authority has been delegated from the CEO. Its purposes are to promote effective decision-making, fix accountability for decisions, and promote managerial teamwork. The check chart allows everyone to see their own role and the roles of everyone else in the decision-making process.

First, each member of the management team identifies his or her top three or four areas of responsibility and indicates who has to assist in the decision making and who has to approve. On the check chart, all of the managers who bear some degree of responsibility are listed in the vertical columns at the top, and the functional areas at the bottom. On the right, each manager is scored as having conditional responsibility, an assisting role, or responsibility for final approval.

Once every manager has completed this personal assessment, each reads his checklist aloud, so that everyone can hear where everyone else is coming from. Review and discussions follow. The list as amended is put to bed. Then we take it a step further to ensure that no area is overlooked. Here we use the *Checklist on Typical Management Responsibilities*, breaking the process down into functional areas such as sales, purchasing, R&D, accounting.

Compared with the conventional job description approach — often hidden in a drawer and outdated — the Check Chart is simple to post, read, review, and adjust as needs be.

In completing the process, the organization will have identified its total tasks, who is *responsible* in each functional area, who must *assist*, and who has *approving authority*.

The list is also read aloud, and we ask what insights the managers have arrived at. "Holy smokes," I heard one participant say. "I realize now that I have to coordinate with every person in here!" We go down the list, seeking loose ends in each area that need to be tied up.

Our clients often find that their big lack is communication. Departments are just not in touch with each other. Each will look at the issues in their own language: engineering, sales, finance, profit, and so on. But perhaps nobody covered R&D or information systems, legal or community relations. The check chart brings everyone into the Big Picture.

CHECK CHART FOR MANAGEMENT ACTION

ORGANIZATION _____

DATE _____

SECTION	Supersedes:

This chart reflects the extent to which authority for decision-making has been delegated from the Chief Executive Officer in order to take necessary management action.

X ——— **Responsible for success or failure of function and has necessary authority after consultation and approval as may be indicated.**

☐ ——— **Assists - this position must be contacted for assistance in formulating program or making decisions.**

O ——— **Approves - decision must be approved by this position before implementation.**

SMALL BUSINESS MANAGEMENT
Leadership
CHECK LIST ON TYPICAL
MANAGEMENT RESPONSIBILITIES*

A.   **General Management**
Business strategy
Growth/Profit Objective
Long-Range Goals
Short-Range Objectives
Performance Plan
Policies
Acquisition/Divestiture
New Sites
Idle Assets
Return on Shareholder Equity

B.   **Financial**
Strategies/Plans
Financial Investment
Financial Statements
Loans
Cash Flow
Credit
Capital Expenditures
Stockholder Relations
Investment Community
Property/Casualty Insurance
Annual Report

C.   **Marketing**
Strategies/Plans
New Markets
Product/Service Profitability
Product/Service Introduction
Distribution Channels
Advertising
Packaging
Selling Price/Discounts
Warranties

D.   **Sales**
Strategies/Plans
Sales Quotas
Sales Coverage
Key Accounts
Sales Promotion
Distribution
Brokers/Distributors
Presentations/Proposals
Trade Shows
Customer Relations
Sales Training

E.   **Distribution**
Strategies/Plans
Service
Delivery
Scheduling
Warehouse

F.   **Organization**
Strategies/Plans
Board of Directors
Executive Committee
Reporting Relationships
Succession Planning
Management Development
New Functions
New Jobs
Communication
Management Trainees

* Note: Check List is designed to serve only as thought simulators in deciding major decision areas with high degree of interaction between functions.

G. **Manufacturing/Operations**
Strategies/Plans
Requirements/Standards
Technical/Engineering Services
Quality Control
Facilities/Equipment
Inventory Management
Scheduling
Order Processing

H. **Purchasing**
Strategies/Plans
Purchase Contract
Supplier Relations

I. **Research & Development**
Strategies/Plans
New Products/Services
New Technology
New Materials
Standards/Testing
Additions/Deletions

J. **Human Resources/Personnel**
Strategies/Plans
Personnel Policies
Manpower Budget
Recruitment - Exempt
Recruitment - Non-Exempt
Orientation
Training
Compensation
Incentive Plans
Employee Benefits
Employee Services
Employee Recognition
Union

K. **Accounting**
Strategies/Plans
Operating Budget
Capital Budget
Statements
Chart of Accounts
Operating Reports
Internal Auditing

L. **Tax**
Liaison with IRS
Tax Returns

M. **Office Management**
Payroll
Procedures
Supplies/Equipment
Site Utilization
Services

N. **Information System**
Strategies/Plans
Information Requirements
Systems Design
Information Processing
New Technology
Equipment Purchase/Lease
Output Reporting

O. **Legal**
Contracts
Licenses/Leases
Patents/Trademarks/Copyrights

P. **Public & Community Relations**
Image
Publicity
Contributions

Working Together: *Trust, Loyalty, and Mutual Respect*

My wife, Marilyn, and I began our business career in consulting more than twenty years ago. People are constantly impressed by our working relationship. We're together all the time, at the office, at home, having fun, and whatever happens, we always seem to take it in stride.

We've managed to keep our marriage and our professional lives in balance, and we put constant effort into keeping current in our field. We believe in being physically and mentally fit, and we travel for business and pleasure.

Because we enjoy our work and each other, our team approach improves our organizational effectiveness. Positive results with individuals and organizations are passed around by word of mouth.

But many couples have tried to go into business together and found that it just didn't work. Why are we so successful in working together? The answer is quite simple, and it is the secret of success in all organizations and relationships — *mutual trust and mutual respect.*

There are other reasons for our effective personal and business teamwork. Among them, we:

- *Divide up the tasks according to our strengths.*
- *Identify the right clients.*
- *Pay close attention to cash flow.*
- *Have a marketing plan and budget.*
- *Realize that competition with each other is destructive.*
- *Share household duties.*
- *Keep a positive attitude.*
- *Have mutual goals, values and vision.*
- *Know exactly why we're in business.*
- *Understand that constant energy is a necessity.*
- *Know that innovation sparks energy.*

In a partnership of any kind, play to your strong suits. One couple we will call the Smiths ran a small business together. Eventually they had to face the fact that Mrs. Smith ruffled customers' feathers so much that people refused to deal with her. Mr. Smith, ever the diplomat, persuaded her to manage the back room while he took care of the customers. He was able to save face for his wife while meeting and resolving customer complaints. The business was saved and now is flourishing.

Trust, loyalty, and *mutual respect* are the keys to success. Also, you absolutely have to avoid playing games for your own advantage, which is office politics.

You Have to Make it through the Flak

Both of the value statements we presented in chapter two from two highly successful companies stressed the importance of holding office politics to the minimum human nature will allow. To me, politics, dissension, conflict, misunderstanding, and lack of communication are all dangerous impediments to getting the job done — like the flak we had to fly through on so many combat missions. This does not rule out healthy and essential differences that surface.

In combat, flak was real and deadly. It filled the air with puffs of black smoke, sometimes so thick it seemed as if you could walk on it. It came at you in hot, jagged pieces of steel that could knock you out of the sky in a second. The first time you saw it, you had a chilling realization: "Hey, these guys are trying to *kill* me!" That was up high, where the 88s were firing. Down below you were in the sights of twin 40 mm cannon. Near the ground, every rifle and machine-gun the Germans had was opening up on you.

But we had to stay on course, jinking and trying to outguess the gunners as best we could, to complete our mission. If we diverted from our task and went after the guns, we might very well not make it to our target. And hitting the target was the entire reason for all of the incredible planning and preparations that had gone into bringing us so far.

Human relationships in any situation are never going to be ideal. Somebody is always looking for an advantage, however large or small. Whatever is going on — a clash of egos or ambitions, deceit, distrust, skulduggery, or just plain bad luck — don't let it divert you from the mission.

It takes resourcefulness to deal with every challenge, so that you can stay on course and reach your target. If you're attacked *ad hominum,* don't get dragged down into the mud. Find the courage and emotional control to stand above petty conflict. To stay angry with someone is to hand them control of your life. Try to relax and smile, no matter how hard that may be. Ignore the flak as best you can and keep on going. You've got a larger purpose.

CHAPTER

THE RESTLESS QUEST FOR CONTINUOUS IMPROVEMENT

Show me a thoroughly satisfied man and I will show you a failure.
Thomas Edison

Strategic Focus

I had just made a bombing strike on some armored vehicles in the Falaise Gap and was down low, skimming the treetops, when the earth erupted in front of my airplane. My P-47 "Jug" slammed into a shock wave and was slapped upward like a toy as I flew through the smoke and flying debris of a great explosion.

Shaking my head to clear the fog from my brain, I looked up and saw the split tail of an American P-38 in a slight climb at about 4,000 feet. It was the only plane in the sky. Down below was an open field, so what that guy was trying to hit, I'll never know. He had obviously punched his bombs off so high that he couldn't pinpoint anything, and that lit my fuse in a hurry. I was scared and madder than hell.

Without thinking, I jammed on full throttle, kicked in War Emergency Power, and headed for a P-38 victory. I'm not really sure what I was going to do, but I was determined to scare the hell out of him. I was closing on him fast, and it wasn't until I had climbed about 2,000 feet that my cooler side began to take charge. Then I winged over and dove away, grateful for what Lincoln called "the better angels of our nature."

Among the lessons I learned in combat was this:

Pinpoint any target you go after.
Scattering your shot will never get the job done.
In fact, it may work against you.

The opposite of scattering your shot is to carefully target your approach. A computer software company we have worked with since its inception has been tremendously successful for many reasons, but key among these is its *targeted approach*. The corporation follows a carefully developed game plan, choosing a product mix that is specifically tailored to the needs of a well-defined customer base.[1]

Resisting the impulse to follow high-tech fads, the company concentrates on its area of expertise and its purpose — to solve the customer's problems rather than merely to sell products. Sales reps have to learn the customer's business. Using a sophisticated customer profile, they look for prospects who meet their parameters and have critical problems that threaten their survival. They choose the companies they can help as carefully as they choose the products they offer. Their goal, with this precise strategic targeting, is to create long-term, profitable relationships with their clients.

> *Skills for success change daily and dramatically. Yesterday's best is no longer competitive today. Track and field and computers present great examples of this, with records for speed and power being broken on a daily basis. Products and even entire classes of products become obsolete, often in less than a year. Unfortunately, the skills to deploy and use those technologies become obsolete in the same way. This is our challenge.*
>
> *Those whose whole makeup is geared to continually "raising the bar" while surfacing new breakthrough approaches find gratification in a deeply rewarding way. Beyond marketplace returns (recognition, monetary awards, and promotions), as significant as they are, perhaps the greatest reward is to pass on that stimulating mind and heart legacy to their children and grandchildren.*
>
> **Will Shook**
> **Vice President of Sales and Marketing**
> **Strategic Technologies, Inc.**

Personal and Professional Focus: A Higher Order

In our management consulting over the last twenty years, Marilyn and I have pioneered a unique plan-of-action for sharpening focus. It has had a profound impact on organizations, management teams, and individuals. We call it the *R.O.A.D. Map.* The program is built around a core workshop that can be given at any level, from employees and their families to the chief executive officer. An integrated process for defining mission and goals and achieving peak performance, it provides a comprehensive view of where you are and where you're going.

One of the reasons the R.O.A.D. Map is unique is because of its "whole person" approach that covers personal goals as well as career planning. Its objective is to achieve balance and fulfillment in all areas of life. Within an organization, it also bridges the gap between the organization and the individual. For the organization, it zeros in on mission, strategies, and goals and ensures the highest return on human resources. Individuals benefit from taking charge of their own careers and lives, from assessing their talents and strengths, and from measuring their personal growth.

The acronym, R.O.A.D, stands for Results, Organization, Assets, and Development. Under *Results,* you ask yourself what you want to accomplish, why it's important, and how you and the organization will benefit. For *Organization,* you define the organization, public or private sector, and the customers toward whom you're going to target your action. *Assets* is a listing of the people, resources, expertise, and success patterns you will have to draw on. *Development* is planning ahead on what will be done, how, when, and so forth.

Notice that the *Mission* statement is at the top of the chart. We want our clients to define the mission statement first, because from it flow the goals and objectives. Getting at the mission is not a simple process. We go through a number of brain-stretching exercises that allow you to look at your values and what you really want in life before you make any attempt to define the mission.

Another unique aspect of the R.O.A.D. Map process is that in these exercises, and in producing the map itself, we engage the right-brain, emotional and feeling side, as well as the intellect. We have all participants fill out a "coat of arms," for example, drawing in and coloring their concepts of how they see themselves right now, how others see them, how they would *like* to see them-

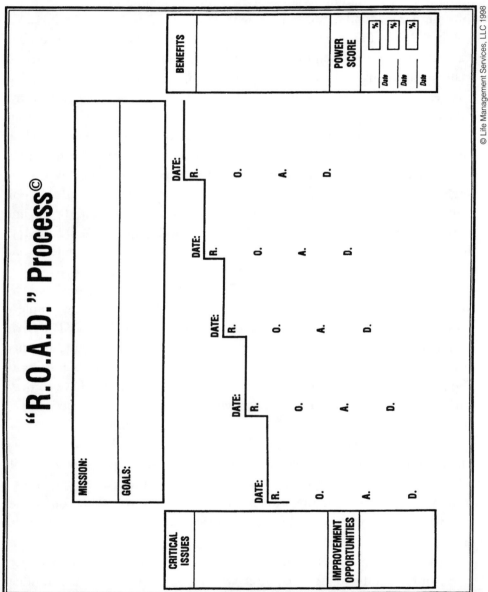

selves, and how they would like the world to see them. Getting the creative process going makes the experience more vivid and, by reaching deeper into ourselves, more profound. The left brain sees the trees and the right brain, the forest. The integrated approach balances head and heart.

Group interaction is also important. There are many points in the workshop at which individuals explain their thoughts to the whole group, providing the reinforcement of both performance and feedback. This participation on the part of the "whole person" creates pride in the end result. At one federal agency, we initially ran into resistance to sharing anything with the group as a whole. As a consequence, only one person from each table was supposed to stand up and present that group's final plan. But by the time people had created their own imaginative layout and plan and discussed it within their small group, everyone wanted to make a presentation.

Beneath the mission statement on the work sheet are the major *Goals*, deriving from the mission, that you want to accomplish. Here again, these aren't just jotted down. Like the mission statement, they evolve through coming at questions from different directions. We challenge you to look at your goals in the areas of Profession/Vocation, Finances, Family, Personal Life, and Recreation and Leisure and to make some definition of your Living Philosophy.

Under the mission and goals are specific, time-phased goals and objectives. The stairstep design gives you a visual image of separate time periods for short, medium, and long range. The planning, in the first phase is precise; planning in the long term, which is three to five or more years out, is much less detailed. The box on the left, *Critical Issues*, is for listing any factors that will impact on your planning and progress in any area and for indicating opportunities to improve. The *Benefits* column on the right is for you to think through and list everything good that will come out of achieving your goals.

The final plan of action that you produce stems from the data on your work sheet and is a unique expression of yourself. Your R.O.A.D. Map is in the general stairstep format in the chart above, but you produce it on a large sheet of flip-chart paper, in all the colors of the rainbow. We have, in fact, seen just about any design you could imagine: rainbows, multi-colored balloons, bridges, and snow-capped mountains.

The R.O.A.D. Map process can be applied on three levels: (1) for an individual, (2) for an organization, or (3) combining individual and organizational goals into a growth and success plan. This latter method, which blends both individual and organizational levels, creates a meaningful end product.

We often do a group map which might be prepared by a complete section of an organization, with thirty to forty people participating. The action plan they produce together shows where the organization is going. It helps when each section or team presents its R.O.A.D. Map action plan to the other groups, so that everyone can see where everyone else is going. When we do the map on an individual basis, people can see the direction others would like to go and what those others hold to be important. This understanding further strengthens bonds among team members and brings the team ever closer to alignment.

The R.O.A.D. Map process has provided an opportunity for many people, as individuals and as team members, to take a deep look at what they believed and where they were going in life. For almost all of them it has been a truly profound, if not a life-changing experience. In a federal agency where we had done team building six years ago, a R.O.A.D. Map was recently spotted, still hanging in an employee's work station. To us, that's evidence that the process was significant then and that it is still significant today.

One graduate of the workshop considers the map process to be a *bridge* between personal and professional goals. Robert Parrott, director of sales and marketing at Zipcom Corporation, has said that most people have both kinds of goals, but they never blend the two. The R.O.A.D. process, he said, defines *"A HIGHER ORDER — A LIFE MEANING."* He didn't know anyone who could focus totally on the professional part of his or her life and say, "This makes me happy." Personal and professional all come full circle, and what makes people happy is "success in all areas of their lives." "R.O.A.D. is out in left field," he said. "Until you've been through it, you have no understanding of the power and success of that program."

This is the mission statement from Robert Parrott's map:

Welcome each day with laughter and understanding,
Challenge each day for balance, purpose, and wisdom,
Cherish each day for the fulfillment of life's true meaning.

Dr. Neila Smith is medical director and director of operations for a leading pharmaceutical contract research organization. When she came to this country some years ago, she said, "I didn't know how to present myself." At that time she had already been the first woman director for an international pharmaceutical company and administrator of a large hospital in India. But coming from an Asian culture in which it is considered arrogant to call attention to oneself, she found it difficult to talk about her achievements. After going through the R.O.A.D. Map process, she said, "I realized that I had to talk a little more about what I'd done. It also helped me to focus on the fact that *if you have knowledge and know how to present it, your opportunities are limitless.*"

> *R.O.A.D. was especially good for heavily left-brain people — to come up with a product that the left brain can handle. As they go into it, it seems touchy-feely, and their response is, "I don't do touchy-feely."*
>
> *I'm a left-brain person who likes to have things laid out and go right down the line. I sometimes work with "butterfly people" who flit from one task to another, and I may have to grab them and keep them there until the job is completed. R.O.A.D. challenged me because I had to go to the right-brain side and jump out of sequence. It's challenging and rewarding to let the creative side come out.*
>
> **James C. Cain**
> **Information Systems Director**
> **U.S. Government**

Attention Control: Performing to Your Full Potential

In dive-bombing, to hit a target as small as a tank, you peeled off from about 5,000 feet, dove almost straight down, and then released your bombs at the last moment. Everything depended upon that split second. You had to ignore the tracers coming up at you, hold your entire concentration on the target, and wait for the exact point that you knew in your gut was right.

In our business and personal life, we sometimes need this intense, narrow focus to avoid distractions, as in problem solving. But to perform effectively in different situations, we have to be able to shift our focus. To see the Big

Picture and conduct planning, we need a broad external focus, like the glow from a lighthouse rather than the beam of a searchlight.

Learning to focus attention for more effective performance was developed in sports, where the results of good or poor concentration are immediate and obvious. Dr. Robert Nideffer, one of the country's top sports psychologists, developed a system called *Attention Control Training* (ACT) to help athletes perform at their optimum level.[2] He has extended ACT into the worldwide business arena in a program for helping individuals gain control over their concentration and people skills.

Nideffer divides attentional focus into four quadrants: broad-internal, broad-external, narrow-internal, and narrow-external. Each of these modes is appropriate for a particular situation. To perform up to our full potential, we have to be in control of our concentration and be able to shift as circumstances demand.

Attention Control Training (ACT)

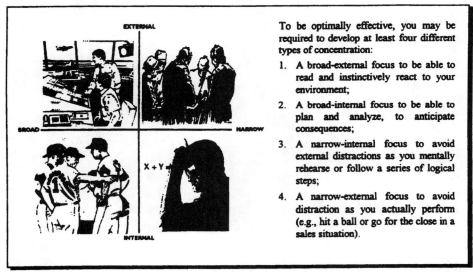

To be optimally effective, you may be required to develop at least four different types of concentration:

1. A broad-external focus to be able to read and instinctively react to your environment;

2. A broad-internal focus to be able to plan and analyze, to anticipate consequences;

3. A narrow-internal focus to avoid external distractions as you mentally rehearse or follow a series of logical steps;

4. A narrow-external focus to avoid distraction as you actually perform (e.g., hit a ball or go for the close in a sales situation).

Courtesy Robert Nideffer

Nideffer found that one factor distinguishing great players from their colleagues was "court sense," the ability to anticipate where the puck or the open man would be. In business terms, this is an instinct that tells a top salesperson, for example, when it is time to close, a "gut level" feeling that resides in the ability to develop a *broad-external focus* of attention.

Business managers also need the ability to think analytically for long-range planning and prioritizing. This skill is part of a *broad-internal focus.*

A *narrow-internal focus* is necessary for avoiding distractions in mental rehearsal, as in the concentration of Olympic diver Greg Louganis, who hit his head on the platform in the middle of an early round dive, then came back and qualified for the finals. On the next day, he won the Olympic Gold Medal in the same dive.

For coming through under great pressure, in highly competitive situations, we need a *narrow-external focus.* This is the ability to concentrate on performing a task amidst external distractions, such as phones ringing and interruptions, or internal distractions like the much lamented "paralysis by analysis."

ATTENTION CONTROL TRAINING is a three step process.

ACT I is to become aware of your current tendencies through taking a 144-item self-report, *The Attentional & Interpersonal Style (TAIS) Inventory,* which Nideffer developed as a tool for applications from executive coaching to employee screening and selection. Based on twenty-five years of research, TAIS measures the way you concentrate, your distractibility, and your tendency to become inflexible, as well as your interpersonal skills, such as preference for diversity, need to control, and self-esteem. By sensitizing you to your most likely mistakes, it serves as an early warning system so that you can make adjustments to maintain control and avoid the difficulty. Most people we have worked with profit immensely from this stage alone.

ACT II is *"centering"* — a learned technique to gain control over your relaxation responses. The goal is to practice breathing and muscle relaxation so that you can bring your tension under control within one or two deep breaths. Centering helps you master performance anxiety and reestablish self-control when you're in danger of losing it.

ACT III emphasizes practice, especially mental rehearsal. Mental rehearsal is more vivid to the senses after good relaxation or centering. But practice makes perfect only if the practice is the right kind. From stage one, the assessment of your tendencies or awareness, you know *what* to rehearse, and from stage two you have the *knowhow,* or the preliminary techniques. Practice puts it together and makes it work.

Find a Better Way

TRANSITIONAL LEADERSHIP

If you could follow a majestic "V" of Canada geese, you would see that the formation regularly changes leadership. The apparent leader, the one flying at the front, will fall back to become a follower, and a follower will move forward to take up the leadership position. The reason for this is apparently that the bird at the apex of the formation takes the brunt of the wind resistance and tires faster than the others. So at any moment in time, the leadership of the flight may be in transition.

Everybody is a leader at one time or another. When a team needs to focus on a particular problem or area of expertise, the person who is most knowledgeable in that area, regardless of his or her position, steps in and provides leadership for as long as it is needed. This transitional leadership enhances creativity and productivity by bringing to bear the most capable and appropriate human resources at the right time and place.

KEEPING UP WITH INFORMATION — A TEAM EFFORT

Both Stephen Covey and Peter Senge stress the importance of expending time and effort to stay abreast of the latest in your field. Covey tells of a man who was taking forever to cut a tree because his saw was dull, but he did not have the time to stop and sharpen it. Covey calls this concept "Sharpen the Saw."[3]

To stay out in front, you have to keep up with current information and developments that could affect your operations. But keeping up on everything you need to know would leave little time for anything else. Turn to the team for help. Decide among yourselves who will be responsible for staying current on a particular subject area and keeping the rest of the team advised. Using team resources in this way multiplies a leader's effectiveness.

DO IT NOW

As a leader, you're always upgrading your skills to find a better way. Many years ago, I learned to practice and teach the concepts of time management and came up with the acronym, *DIN*, for Do It Now. This means that you deal with a situation immediately and don't put it off. When a piece of paper comes across your desk, do something about it NOW! Don't handle the same piece of paper twice. Take action and move on.

These are the options for taking action. Whatever you decide, do something.

Do It
Delegate It
Defer It
Dump It

The rule holds for teams as well as for individuals. The point is to do what's necessary, right now, so that you can clear the decks and go on to the next task.

Go Fishing

You can get going so fast, be so busy, and get so snowed under that you find yourself paddling like hell and going nowhere. You stay late in the office, and still you can't catch up. Eventually you're overwhelmed. Now, in your frustration, you're beginning to feel paralyzed, and your output *really* drops. You're falling even farther behind.

That description is a little melodramatic, but you get the point. We have all been overwhelmed at times. If you get wound up too deeply in your work and its problems, you're not going to have the vision to be productive. To be truly creative, you have to be at peace.

When you're up to your ears in alligators, take a break. *Go fishing.* Let everything settle back into perspective. I realize this is not so easy when you're pressed hard, because relaxing seems like a waste of precious time. But what you're really doing is allowing your wellspring to refresh itself. Give your inner self time to come up with some answers. Let your right brain kick in and restore your vision.

When I went into a full court press to solve the problems of the 50th Fighter Wing at Hahn Air Base in Germany, I had to let a lot of things go. The papers built and built and built on my desk. I was just getting nowhere, so I called one of the squadrons and said, "Hey, give me a bird," and lined up an F-100 Super Sabre Jet fighter for a low-level flight into France. Nothing in the world relaxed me like flying.

Just after I lifted off from our runway above the Mosel River, my troubles began to drop away. Soon I was whipping along on the deck, and with the habit I had learned in combat, kept my head on a swivel, watching the skies for other aircraft.

After a while I saw a speck in the sky, high and to the rear, at about the 4:30 position. It was a fighter, closing on me fast. His intention was clearly to jump me and pass like a bat out of hell, waggling his wings, which meant, "Gotcha. You're dead."

He was gaining on me at a pretty good overtake speed. I held my heading until he was almost in gun range, so he wouldn't know I had spotted him. Then I kicked my bird and honked it straight up. He tried to follow, but he was going too fast and overshot me. As he scrambled for altitude, I flipped over and rolled down on his tail. The hunter had become the hunted.

That pilot tried every imaginable maneuver to get away, but I turned inside him and closed the distance until I was glued to his rear end. Then I pulled up in formation on his right wing. The plane was a French F-100 with tricolor markings. As I waved and peeled off for home, I was in Fighter Pilot Heaven.

Flying back, priorities on the work I'd left behind became clear. After landing, I went through my papers and projects like wildfire. My mind was no longer cluttered by so many things undone, and I had a whole new outlook.

Find what works for you. Go outside and do something you like, practice breathing exercises, yoga, meditation, take a walk. The point is to get away from the routine that has bogged you down. When you're stuck, you'll most likely keep doing the same thing over and over. Shift your perspective.

Keep a Logbook

Dr. Win Wenger, a pioneer in the study of human intelligence, has noted that the information we have about many great men is so extensive because they left detailed records of their thoughts. Among these are Ben Franklin's *Autobiography*, Einstein's *Autobiographical Notes*, and Leonardo da Vinci's *Notebooks*. This "compulsive scribbling," he indicates, may be part of what made them great.[4]

As a young student in Zurich, Albert Einstein used to sail with his comrades on the Zurichsee. A companion noticed that every time the wind died, Einstein would take out a notebook and start writing. When the sails filled, he put the notebook away and went back to sailing. No one knows what he wrote, but Wenger says, "It can hardly be an accident that researchers in the field of high intelligence have long regarded the habit of compulsive scribbling as one of the telltale hallmarks of genius."

Was their writing simply a product of a highly inflated ego? Wenger argues that the writing was, in and of itself, "a mechanism by which people who were not born geniuses unconsciously nurtured and achieved a superior intellect."

He also cites research on an order of nuns who condemned the sin of mental idleness and allowed their brains no downtime. They lived much longer than average and were unusually resistant to brain diseases that afflict the elderly: Alzheimer's, stroke, and dementia. Ceaseless activity apparently kept the channels open and the circuits strong.

An Indian tribe that allowed its infants to crawl freely had a twenty-five-point higher IQ level than one that restrained them. The difference was in the sensory feedback they received from their own spontaneous self-expression. This "expression circuit," Wenger indicates, is more responsible for the brain's physical development than genetic inheritance.

That's fancy reasoning for keeping a log. As far as I'm concerned, writing things down helps to sort them out. Once you have expressed yourself in writing, you have taken a stand: "This is where I am right now." In the swift flow of life the next thought, committed to paper, is another stand, and it becomes another building block. Declaring ourselves to ourselves helps us know where we have been, where we are, and where we are going.

Continuous Improvement: The Endless Pursuit of Quality

Maybe you can't find the perfect fix, the magic solution, the silver bullet. Maybe your organization doesn't have a game plan that will automatically catapult it to success. Not many of us do. It's a tough world out there, and what we get we generally earn the hard way.

However, no matter how clear or obscure your direction, there is one activity to which you can always devote your energies with confidence that you are making a well-justified investment in your future. As I have said before, you never, never, never stop looking for a better way of doing things. The quest for continuous improvement is the ongoing part of the process I have laid out in this book. It never ends. You don't have to see how to climb the mountain all at once. Just keep doing what you're doing, better and better, and you'll get there.

Continuous improvement and quality go hand in hand. As I have noted, Donald Petersen, former president, chairman, and CEO of Ford Motor Company, was the driving force behind Ford's quality turn-around in the 1980s. In 1990, *Fortune* Magazine named Petersen "The Most Successful Boss Since the Original Henry in His Prime." When Petersen took charge of Ford, Japanese quality and efficiency of production had eclipsed that of the American automobile industry. His solution was, first, to seek continuous improvement. "When I couldn't draw up a plan to make Ford profitable again," he has written, "we did have a lot of ideas how we could make continuous improvements. That became our guide-on, and the rate of financial improvement far exceeded anything our financial people could forecast. It was a great morale booster and vital to our effort."[5]

Number one among Ford's Guiding Principles was this statement:

Quality comes first. To achieve customer satisfaction, the quality of our products and service must be our number-one priority.[6]

Ford put quality first even when it was losing money. To overcome skepticism about the company's commitment to quality over cost-consciousness, the management team had to prove that it practiced what it preached. When it came to a choice between closing a newer plant with an indifferent product or an older one that was devoted to quality, the positive decision went to the plant that gave quality top priority. Petersen said in his book, *A Better Idea*, "This sent a simple message: from that day forward, the plants with the worst quality records would be the first to go."[7] Further, Ford held up the scheduled production run of its new Escort until it worked out the quality problems, and then it held back providing an automatic transmission until they got it right. Management was proving that it meant business.

During the 1980s, Ford began to catch up with and then surpass a good number of the Japanese companies in the area of quality. The secret of their success, Petersen says, was not some magical breakthrough in design or technology, but rather, "steadiness of purpose: empowering people and buying into the idea of continuous improvement." He adds that "The secret is making steady progress in everything you do."[8]

But quality should not be too narrowly defined. As the Ford management team looked more deeply into the company's purpose, they began to realize that they had to take into account not only the object measurement of what was wrong, but also people's judgments about what was right. They had to like the look and feel. The company had to appeal to its customers, both internal and external.

Therefore, the second of Ford's Guiding Principles began with the statement, *"Customers are the focus of everything we do,"* and up front in its Mission Statement is this commitment: *"... to improve continually our products and services to meet our customer's needs...."* [9]

Finally, as I have reiterated so many times, it all comes down to people. To revitalize its work force, Ford launched an employee involvement program to "take advantage of the know-how of everyone in the company, not just the people at the top." "Employee involvement teams" began to meet regularly to discuss ways to improve operations and the work environment. Over the years the teams contributed "tens of thousands of highly worthwhile ideas...." "Without those ideas," Petersen writes, "the company's revitalization would have been impossible." [10]

Continuous improvement, which is the endless pursuit of quality, depends upon creating the kind of synergistic interaction among people that can make tremendous quality improvements by tapping the power of teamwork. Like spirit, continuous improvement just seems to flow in an organization that's aligned around a core of deep inner values, with human beings at all levels working together in a positive and nurturing environment.

CHAPTER

HOLDING ON TO SUCCESS

Success is never final; failure is never fatal.
Winston Churchill

Don't Let Success Go To Your Head

The motto of the NATO military headquarters in Belgium is this: *"Eternal Vigilance is the Price of Liberty."* For a business or professional organization, the price of sustained peak performance is eternal vigilance in continually redefining what it believes and what it does. It is also in the degree to which it respects its people and is able to unite them in a common cause.

The greatest enemy of success is complacency.

No matter how well you have done, or how good you feel about your organization, or how bright your prospects, you can't afford to sit still. While you fixate on doing the same thing, over and over, somebody else has found a better way and is coming up with something new. You're going to be blindsided, like IBM, when it failed to anticipate the runaway PC market, and General Motors, when it ignored Japanese quality.

A great organization is always characterized by its ability to embrace *change* and its ceaseless pursuit of finding a new and better way: the restless quest for continuous improvement.

Four years ago we were in a brainstorming session with a small company which at that time had twenty-seven people and an $8 million gross annual revenue. The company was only a few years old, but it was growing rapidly and building a solid base. The topic at hand concerned challenges and opportunities. Questions were, "What can we build on?" and "What must we overcome?"

This was the first input: *"Don't let success go to your head." "Continue to learn and grow." "No one has all the answers."*

With those principles firmly anchored in the corporate culture, the firm has since grown to about 100 people with an annual gross of more than $50 million.

True success is continual. It is not hitting the perfect note, but it is the continuous combination of perfect notes that create a song. Holding on to success and establishing it as part of one's makeup requires that people savor their victories and smell the roses, because that's what makes the taste for the next success so stimulating. Along with the desire for achievement, success demands the desire for never-ending improvement and excellence in execution.

Lasting success is not something you accomplish in life independently. It requires teamwork and sharing success with others. Therefore, it also requires understanding others, their desires, and capabilities, and creating roles and challenges that allow people to be successful in their own right. Finally, you have to be able to "read the tea leaves" to stay on the success vector as it changes its trajectory. You have to understand the changing world around us and be able to adapt to the fundamental shifts that occur continuously.

The Life Cycles of a Corporation

A company that has made it to the top, no matter how dizzying the heights, has no guarantee that it will stay there. Like people, organizations can suffer from a hardening of the arteries and lose the innovative spirit that made them great. After the exit of its co-founders, including Steve Jobs, Apple Computer began to lose its sure sense of direction and youthful spirit, eventually falling on hard times.

But even though an organization can go through a life cycle similar to that of a human being, from infancy to peak performance and then to decline and death, the process is not inevitable. This is the finding of Dr. Ichak Adizes, who has laid out ten stages of corporate life cycles in his book, *The Pursuit of Prime.*

"Prime" is the stage at which organizations, like people, are at their healthiest and most productive. "Prime is not a destination," he says. "It is a condition."[1] This is a time when the organization has undergone all of the developmental stages and now enjoys a magic balance between flexibility and control.

Adizes lists the ten stages of corporate life cycles as:

- *Courtship*
- *Infancy*
- *Go-Go*
- *Adolescence*
- *Prime*
- *Stability*
- *Aristocracy*
- *Recrimination*
- *Bureaucracy*
- *Death*

Courtship is the time of dreaming and becoming committed to the dream. *Infancy* begins when the founder shifts from ideas to results, which in the business world means producing sales. The next stage, *Go-Go*, is a time of rapid growth and opportunity, with the founders continuing to make all the decisions and becoming arrogant in their new success. These are the Developing Stages.

The first of the Coming-of-Age Stages is *Adolescence*, in which the company faces uncontrolled growth, internal conflict, and a temporary loss of vision. If the organization develops controls without losing flexibility, it passes into the next state, *Prime*. In this ideal situation, the company is innovative, yet disciplined. It meets its customers' needs and spins off new organizations.

Aging begins with *Stability*, a stage in which excitement fades, financial officers start focusing on short-term gains, and energy and innovation wane. *Aristocracy* is the next phase, when perks, titles, and forms become all-important. Cash-rich, the corporation acquires companies (and stifles them) rather than creating new businesses. In the *Recrimination* stage, the company looks for scapegoats to blame for the mess it's in and will cut people to trim costs, rather than finding ways to increase revenues.

The penultimate stage is *Bureaucracy*, in which the organization focuses on its internal hierarchy and stops caring about satisfying its customers. Rules and policies stifle innovation and creativity. The final stage, *Death*, may come swiftly, or it may take years, but it becomes inevitable when the organization can no longer generate the cash it needs to meet its obligations.

Adizes, who refers to himself as an "organizational therapist," emphasizes that once companies reach prime, they do not necessarily have to leave it. They can even return to their peak from a state of decline. It is doubtful that they can do this on their own, since those who would do the fixing are probably the people who got the organization into such a mess in the first place — but help is available. Whether it is staying at the top or returning to days of glory, the effort requires both highly dedicated leadership and eternal vigilance.

Three Essentials for Keeping an Organization Great

It is my firm conviction that there are three major ingredients for continuing corporate growth and success. The first of these is *alignment*, which we saw in chapter nine as having to do with people, values, and the kind of relationship that promotes synergy in a team or organization. Alignment is a precondition to the second essential for continued success, which is *innovation*. This does not mean innovation as a flash in the pan, but as an active, ongoing method of operation. Without continuous innovation, there will likely be no breakthrough performance. The third essential factor is *business imperatives*, of which the all-important area of financial skills is a major part.

Creating Great Organizations

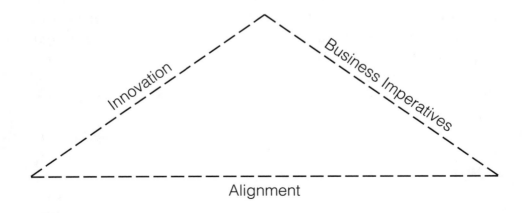

Alignment: The Foundation
THE INSEPARABILITY OF PROFESSIONAL AND PERSONAL LIFE

Alignment has another facet. It is also about balancing and blending the two worlds of our lives: *personal and professional.* Try as we may, we can't separate the two. What affects one, positively or negatively, affects the other. They are as tightly intertwined as the two hemispheres of our brains.

Watch, as I have, when someone has suddenly become deprived of a major part of the left hemisphere. The result is a devastating loss of the ability to communicate through speech or writing. Think of using your left leg at work and the right one at home. Ridiculously limiting. But so is the strategy within those organizations which focus solely on the professional lives of their people and give little, if any, attention to the personal side.

Forward-looking CEOs, managers, and team leaders who recognize that these two sides of our lives feed on one another take measures to foster growth and understanding in both the personal and professional areas of employees' lives. Such a program brings significant returns.

In the short term, turnover drops or is avoided, as does employee burnout. Productivity, morale, and worker retention increase. The fact that management *cares* adds positive notes to the corporate culture, and loyalty gains a strong foothold. In the long term, the workers of tomorrow come from the families of today. If CEOs, executive staff, stockholders, and board members intend their companies to be their legacy for the future, they will take responsibility for encouraging family growth and development. It makes good business sense.

Family/work programs are currently being successfully implemented within major corporations, such as NationsBank, Xerox, and Marriott International. These programs make a commitment to promoting healthy family and work life, with benefits such as child and elder care, flexible work schedules, and a variety of policies related to employee and family interests.

Hugh McColl, NationsBank chairman, has said of its family/work program, *"The bank's turnover rate is 50 percent less among the 35,000 employees who have taken advantage of programs designed to help balance work and family life."*

Pam Farr, senior vice president at Marriott International, said, *"Our company's family support program has demonstrated a five-to-one payback for every dollar in terms of lower absenteeism, fewer accidents at work sites, better customer service, and increased employee satisfaction and loyalty."*

A Five-Point Prescription for Alignment

Below are the essentials of a five-point prescription for achieving and maintaining alignment. The *formula has evolved from half a century* of working, observing, learning, and consulting in the worlds of both professional and personal life.

ENLIGHTENED & GROWTH DRIVEN ALIGNMENT

1. TEAM BUILDING & INTERACTION
  "Emotional Intelligence" Base
  Appropriate Instrument(s)

2. DEVELOP ORGANIZATION
  VALUES • MISSION • STRATEGY • GOALS • TACTICS
    All Departments & Echelons
    Convey Via Plans To Which All Have Contributed
    Achieve Through Inter-Active Alignment

Whatever the management techniques, success in the future will go to those organizations in which every member has a personal stake in the outcome.

3. DEVELOP INDIVIDUAL
  VALUES • MISSION • GOALS • TACTICS
    Balance & Blend With Those Of The Organization
    Convey Via Personalized Plan Reflecting Individual & Organization Growth & Success

4. CONTINUALLY SEEK
  To Enhance Performance, i.e., TAIS* & ACT*
  For Vision Toward Better Way

5. LEADERSHIP
  Value Based
  Long Term Vision
  Sincerely & Inspiringly Conveyed
  Relationship Sensitive

*The Attentional & Interpersonal Style (TAIS) Inventory with *Attention Control Training (ACT)
© Life Management Services, LLC 1996

1. TEAM BUILDING AND INTERACTION:

Creating alignment begins with team building. We consistently start with an understanding of Emotional Intelligence, since team building is all about building relationships and trust. The whole becomes greater than the sum of its parts. Alignment evolves over time as the team works, grows, socializes, and has fun together, and as it proceeds through the following steps.

2. ORGANIZATION, VALUES, MISSION, GOALS, TACTICS:

The key here, beyond the doing of it, is to ensure that every member of the organization has a hand in the planning process, with their voices being not only heard, but encouraged. The idea is to bring together the collective strength of the organization.

3. INDIVIDUAL VALUES, MISSION, GOALS, TACTICS:

Establishing individual direction is one of the most meaningful tools for putting the five-point prescription to work. It has a positive impact on team building and sets the stage for leadership to really take off.

To institute such a program is quite easy and takes but a small amount of time and effort, from encouraging that it be done, drawing on the goal-setting experiences from step two (above), to holding half-day workshops and beyond. This concept supports and complements the family/work efforts that are having such a positive impact in corporations today.

4. ENHANCING PERFORMANCE:

Continuing measures are needed to enhance performance in the most relevant ways — to remain not only current, but on the leading edge. The TAIS/ACT combination makes a unique contribution here.

5. LEADERSHIP:

Leadership is exhibited not only by the team leader, but by all members of the team at one time or another. In a rapidly growing organization, team members become the nucleus for expansion and have the opportunity to move into positions of increased authority and responsibility.

Innovation

ALIGNMENT IS THE SETTING

As the essence of bringing up children is to combine structure and discipline with love and understanding (consistent with Dr. James Dobson's book,

Dare to Discipline²), the essence of holding on to organizational success is combining *structure and discipline* with encouraging *innovation*. This is to apply the collective gifts within the organization in a spirit of harmony, trust, and respect.

Within the organization, structure and discipline are "alignment" in every sense of the word. True alignment, as it has been defined in this book, is free of backbiting and politics, insensitive management, and being overly concerned with the product at the expense of people.

Alignment provides the setting in which people are nourished, encouraged, and supported. They're motivated. They care. And from a base of shared values, they are able to put their heart into their job and engage all of their ingenuity in finding a better way of doing things. In many cases, people are creating their own niche, which could become an "intrapreneurship" opportunity. Motivation sparks creativity, and a great source of motivation is the group environment and spirit. It takes a "people" climate to foster outstanding creativity.

"THINK OUT OF THE BOX"

Mike Vance, former head of Disney University and co-author of *Think Out of the Box*, was an infantryman in Korea when he came up with a concept he calls "Kitchen for the Mind."³ This is essentially a setting that encourages creativity. His first "kitchen" was his sleeping bag, which he made into a home by gathering together items dedicated not to the needs of the stomach, but to those of the brain. These were family pictures, books, and writing paper, all of which contributed to stimulating mental activity.

This evolved into the "Team Center" concept in business. The Team Center provides a social gathering place filled with resources to stimulate creative thinking. It is an "enriched place" where people take part in projects, programs, celebrations, and personal activities.

The book's title refers to an exercise in which you have to draw a line outside the confines of the figure in order to connect nine dots. To complete the task takes unconventional thinking. Vance provides some structures to organize creative thought, project development, and implementation.

I believe that this kind of structured approach to creativity can significantly accelerate innovation in a team or corporation. The point here is that *innovation can be structured*. Techniques discussed in Vance's book have been used by Apple Computer, General Electric, AT&T, General Foods, Johnson & Johnson, and the Walt Disney Company. See chapter four: "Creativity."

Organizing Innovation

Nothing characterizes a great company more distinctly than its ability to anticipate trends, see opportunities, come up with new ideas, and, with youthful flexibility, change its course to stay ahead of a changing world. *Continuous innovation is the key to holding on to success.*

Peter Drucker has said that our belief in America's superiority in entrepreneurship is "lulling us into a dangerous complacency," similar to our complacency about management in the 1970s, "just as the Japanese were about to run circles around us in mass production and customer service."[4] A reason for this, he said, is that while we know that entrepreneurship is a rigorous discipline that has to be organized to create a new business, we still believe that *innovation* is largely R&D, which is technical.

We think that innovation is a "flash of genius" and not a systematic, organized, and rigorous discipline. Meanwhile, the Japanese and Koreans have set up small groups to systematically apply the discipline of innovation to identify and develop new products. The key to organizing innovation is *"to systematically identify changes that have already occurred in a business — in demographics, in values, in technology or science — and then to look at them as opportunities."* Systematic innovation also requires a step that is difficult for most companies: "to abandon rather than defend yesterday."

Drucker states emphatically that "The large organization has to learn to innovate, or it won't survive." Increasingly, large organizations are growing through alliances and joint ventures, but they don't necessarily know how to work with a partner and determine shared values and goals.

Innovation means "changing your products and services to keep up with markets that are changing faster than anybody has ever seen." The entire banking industry is no longer making money on loans and deposits, as banks have traditionally done, but is now making its profits on credit cards, ATM fees, currency trades, and selling mutual funds.

Large companies can foster entrepreneurship, but they often have to set up an internal unit "that behaves quite differently from the rest of the company." This was the case when General Motors created Saturn as an entity separate from GM's management culture.

The more successful the unit is, he said, the more difficult it is for the company not to place the same expectations on it as it does on the rest of the organization. A new venture, inside or outside the business, is a child, says Drucker, adding: "And you don't put a forty-pound pack on a six-year-old's back when you take her hiking."

> *There are companies that are good at improving what they're already doing…. There are companies that are good at extending what they're doing. And finally there are companies that are good at innovation. Every large company has to be able to do all three — improve, extend, and innovate — simultaneously."*
>
> **Peter Drucker**

"Always Mess with Success"

In their book, *If it ain't broke… BREAK IT!*, Robert J. Kriegel and Louis Patler challenge the conventional wisdom that if something isn't broken, don't fix it.[5] The law of nature is to grow and evolve, and everything around us is in a constant state of change. And since everything exists in relationship to something else, *relationships* are changing as well — whether it's the relationship of a service to a need or a product to a customer. There is no such thing as a finished product.

The only way to survive and triumph is to go out and meet change, welcome it, take it on, wrestle with it, and wherever you can, ambush it, say Kriegel and Patler. We should always question *what is* and never allow complacency to lead us into "plateauing," which happens when someone just goes through the motions and "retires on the job." There's no joy in life when someone has given up and stops growing.

Most organizations, like people, don't change until they have to. When things go badly, they try desperately to find a quick fix, but the problem is that "you don't think clearly with a gun at your head." Trying to play catch-up leads to poor decision making, lack of innovation, and poor morale.

Break It! also has this advice: *"The best time to change is when you don't have to."*

Business Imperatives

Although the concentration of this book is on people, values, and relationships — and nourishing growth and innovation, I would be remiss to overlook the third factor in the triangle: *business imperatives.* Without carefully attending to these operational essentials, a company will be limited to, at best, mediocrity.

Business imperatives encompass a multiplicity of practices, skills, and strategies. These include marketing, sales, CFO activities, and logistics. There is, however, one specific necessity for any organization to realize its full potential: *the art and science of the financial planning process*— having a keen awareness of the numbers, ratios, profit and loss, when to say "yes," and when to say "no." This means that every member of the organization becomes a businessperson. All are pulling together to make a *fair* profit, without which no company can remain in business.

This concept is critical to achieving and sustaining great performance.

Measuring Your Success Rate

No matter how great your current success, you can never *assume* that you're doing all right. You have to know where you stand, what you're doing right and what you're doing wrong, what works and what doesn't work. You have to know where to concentrate your resources and where to back off. Remember the old adage that a chain is no stronger than its weakest link.

At Life Management Services, we have developed a three-step method of taking inventory to show you where your organization stands in terms of alignment, goals, leadership, and teamwork, and to find out how what it's *doing* measures up to what it *should be* doing. These are:

- *The Power Index*
- *The 15-Question Management Checklist*
- *Brainstorming to Identify the Key Problems*

THE POWER INDEX

This index plots a graphic picture of where the organization stands in terms of the four D's — *Desire, Discovery, Direction,* and *Doing.* You are asked to rate your company on a scale of 0 to 10 on how well it performs in each of these four categories. Zero is the lowest rating; ten is the highest. The results are tallied in a Power Score, expressed as a percentage. The Power Score is your report card, as your employees see it, on how well the organization is meeting its potential. The Index serves as an early warning device. If everyone believes you're operating at 50 percent of your capability, or less, it's time to start plugging leaks or look for a lifejacket .

LMS Power Index
(For The Organization)

<u>Profile Chart</u>
Use this chart to plot your organization's-ratings ("X") for each of the growth stages:
DESIRE - DISCOVERY - DIRECTION - DOING.
Connect the "X's" with a line to provide a graphic picture of how you measure your organization.

Rating Scale	DESIRE To what extent are we motivated to be successful?	DISCOVERY To what extent are we utilizing our assets?	DIRECTION To what extent have we defined our missions and goals?	DOING To what extent are we putting forth the energy to "make it happen"?	POWER SCORE
High 10.					300 (100%)
9.					
8.					225 (75%)
7.					
6.					
Medium 5.	— — —	— —	— —	— — —	150 (50%)
4.					
3.					75 (25%)
2.					
1.					
Low 0.					0 (0%)

Compute your Power Score by using this formula:
DESIRE + DISCOVERY + DIRECTION x DOING =
Today [ ] + [ ] + [ ] x [ ] = [ ]

In sports there is no substitute for the sheer determination to go on to the last measure of strength and courage. This quality of *DESIRE* is expressed in the question, "To what extent are we motivated to be successful?" How much do people care? *DISCOVERY* questions how well you're doing with what you have. This is a measure of basic competency and effectiveness. *DIRECTION* asks how well you have defined your missions and goals, and *DOING* asks to what degree you are putting forth the energy to "make it happen." How is your execution?

We find that in an outstanding company, the area singled out as having the greatest opportunity for continued growth is on the *people* side. Because everything else is solid, the organization is able to concentrate on utilizing its greatest asset to seek innovation and new ways of doing things. A company that is operating far below its potential has to take a more basic approach. It has to go all the way back to the beginning and first get its *direction* straight.

FIFTEEN-QUESTION MANAGEMENT CHECKLIST

Immediately before a company's annual mission and goals-setting exercise, we frequently ask everyone to respond to fifteen questions, which are all positive statements covering three critical areas: *Goals, Leadership*, and *Teamwork*. Since the questionnaire is completed by all of the employees, you get an honest profile of how everyone judges your management style and capabilities. If your managers get a low score on teamwork, for example, you're headed for trouble.

The number of times you can say "Yes" tells you where you're doing well and where you have to make changes. Since the ratings have a numerical score, you can quantify the outcome and track your progress from year to year.

BRAINSTORMING TO IDENTIFY THE KEY PROBLEMS

With the issues sorted out in these two questionnaires, we proceed to a brainstorming session to identify the most important problems. We ask, "What are your thoughts?" and "How we can get a handle on this?" Clearly defining the problems is a prelude to redefining values and setting goals. (See "Brainstorming to Find the Best Solution" in chapter four.)

LIFE MANAGEMENT SERVICES, LLC
Consultants in Human Services

301 Gregson Drive, Cary , NC 27511
(919) 481-4707 Fax: (919) 469-4751

MANAGEMENT CHECKLIST:

RATING SCALE
3 = YES
2 = NOT SURE
1 = NO

CAN YOU SAY "YES"?

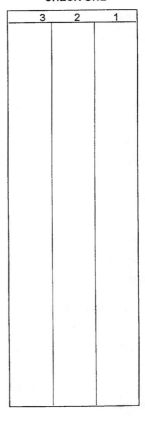

CHECK ONE

3	2	1

Goals

1. Do you feel there is a reasonable meshing of organization and employee *goals*?
2. Do managers and employees *understand* your organization's goals and strategies?
3. Does your organization have a positive *quality* of *worklife*?
4. Is enough time spent planning instead of "firefighting"?
5. Are employees sufficiently trained and motivated to *commit* themselves to your organization's common purpose?

Leadership

6. Is the structure of your organization built around *leadership talents*?
7. Are responsibilities clearly defined with *accountability*?
8. Do your managers set high standards for *performance*?
9. Is *decision-making* and *problem-solving* carried out by those most knowledgeable and closest to the problem?
10. Are your managers willing to take responsible *risks* while meeting present responsbilities?

Teamwork

11. Is your organization able to attract and keep *talented people*?
12. Do your managers work together for *results* as a team?
13. Is top management tuned to *employee thinking*?
14. Are employees recognized and rewarded for *innovation and performance*?
15. Is your organization alive with a "can do" and "will do" attitude?

OVERALL RATING

Develop Your Managers — A 360-Degree View

As the great Scottish poet Robert Burns wrote, what a gift it would be "to see ourselves as others see us."

But there is no magic mirror in which we, as managers, can see our image clearly, from all angles and from all perspectives. Our vision is limited by what we are. Nor can we necessarily expect candor and relevant feedback from our colleagues in the workplace. When we address the real issues of leadership and management, we're talking about the personal skills of getting along with people. And because they're *personal*, we're about as eager to enter that touchy area with others as we are to walk into a minefield.

Each great organization needs a means of developing leadership and managerial skills through *objective feedback, coaching*, and *follow through*. The purpose of assessing managers is not to get rid of them, but rather, to strengthen the organization by bringing out their personal strengths and working on areas that need further development. The key is to approach this assessment in a nonthreatening manner.

To gain a *360-degree* view of how a manager is perceived by himself, his boss, his peers, and those who report to him, for a number of years we have used the Management and Leadership Profile (MLP) developed by Curtiss Peck and provided by Assessment Systems International, Inc.[6] The MLP is a series of 119 items, each of which describes positive leadership and management behavior. The individual is asked to respond in two ways: (1) how *does* the individual perform in this area, and (2) how *should* the person perform? The MLP measures the gap between where individuals think they are and where others, as well as they themselves, think they should be.

The items include operational skills, such as "Establishes specific time frames for measuring our progress toward goal achievement," and people issues such as "Pays attention while listening." The objective is to get an all-around picture that says, "Here's where I am," and "Here's where I should be." Looking at all of the managers from this standpoint and identifying the gaps between what is and what should be gives us an overall profile of the organization.

Here's how it works. Every person rates himself or herself. The individual is also rated by his or her boss or bosses if the individual reports to more than one person. He or she is then rated by four or five peers. Finally, those who report to the individual also provide a rating. To maintain anonymity, there should be at least three direct reports. At a minimum, you need a total of five ratings: you, your boss, and three people who work for you.

Curtiss Peck stresses that it is important to help individuals focus on their strengths first. Their strengths are what they do best, and feeling good about these will help them be more objective in accepting their "soft-spots" and developing plans for improvement. Soft spots (weaknesses) are an absence of a strength rather than something for which people should be criticized.

It's not advisable to use the MLP with just one or a few managers. They need to be seen and to see themselves as part of a larger system. Their future behavior and the positive changes that can come about will result from their interaction within the system.

When we used this assessment a few years ago in an organization that was having some management conflict, it was like opening Pandora's box. The senior manager was a brilliant engineer, but his people skills were in the low to zero range. He told the team, for example, to have a piece of software ready to ship in fifteen days.

"There's no way we can do it right," they said.

"I promised," he said. "Get off your rear and get it done."

It was clear that this project was going to blow up in their faces. Employee reaction ran along these lines: "If that S.O.B. is staying, I'm leaving." That resentment was surfaced in administering the MLP 360-degree instrument. As a result, the engineer was taken out of management and became a high-level consultant, a position in which his strengths could be better utilized.

Even with self-managed teams and greater delegation, employees don't want to be left alone to determine their own fate. People at all levels want and need good management and leadership. The purpose of giving feedback to managers is to develop their skills so that they can provide guidance and inspire the kind of commitment that will allow the organization to grow and change.

Values: The Constant in a World of Change

A key factor in maintaining your direction in a world environment of bewildering change is to have something permanent to hang on to, a source of guidance and inspiration that doesn't change. You're not always going to have all of the information you need to make good decisions; sometimes all you have to rely on are principles that you know in your own experience to be true. This brings us back to one of the central themes of this book: the importance of knowing and living by solid and positive *values*.

Pat Allen, a vice-president with a successful high-tech company, has said that with technology changing so quickly, a product isn't around for more than eighteen months, so in hiring, current skills are less important than values, motivation, and goals. "We can train people in skills," he said. "It is much harder to teach values and motivation."

He spends a lot of time on hires, finding out what they care about in life and their personal and career goals. "Hiring and training is a very expensive proposition," he said. "We just can't afford to make mistakes with our most valuable asset."

An outstanding aspect of the organization's corporate culture is its high degree of alignment between company and personal values, a situation which Pat Allen says is "like a V-8 engine with all the cylinders firing." It is a shared commitment that begins with the hiring stage, continues through a "bottom-up, grass-roots planning process," and is continually expressed in these questions: *"Is what we're doing moving us toward our goals? Is it adding value to the company? Is it adding value to our customers?"*

A Dirty Little Secret — Corporate Hypocrisy

"Today, in the corridors of business as elsewhere, families are getting more lip service than ever.... But corporate America harbors a dirty secret.... Families are no longer a big plus for a corporation; they are a big problem. An albatross." [7] (*Fortune* Magazine, March 17, 1997.)

The cover of Fortune recently featured a toddler clinging to the high-heeled leg of a mother on her way to work, with the story title, "Is Your Family Wrecking Your Career?" *Fortune* senior writer Betsy Morris states in the article that having a wife and three children is no longer a career plus if both spouses work, which is the case for 84 percent of all married couples. Working parents simply won't be available for the single-minded devotion that success in the corporation or the law firm requires. "In a world built on just-in-time, the ideal employee is the one who's always available," she writes, "not the one who's constantly torn."

This is the direct opposite of the work/family approach, which we have seen being successfully tried in major business enterprises. It contradicts the basic philosophy of the new, more enlightened outlook, which is that the more fulfilled workers are in all spheres of their lives, the more productive they become.

The kids, who spend significantly less time with adults than a few decades ago, are increasingly vulnerable to drug and alcohol abuse, failing in school, or getting pregnant. Companies are trying to help, with flexible schedules and some day care, but Morris says the problem is structural: the way work is organized today and the way managerial career paths are structured mean that employees with children lose out. But ultimately, she believes, industry will have to accommodate parents because it can't afford to lose them.

SEEKING QUALITY OF LIFE

On the other hand, the *Wall Street Journal* indicates that corporate recruiters have seen a trend among undergraduates toward raising questions of life/work balance in employment interviews.[8] In talks with recruiters for twelve big employers, writer Sue Shellenbarger found students raising such questions as, "Do people who work for you have a life off the job?" and "Do your employees get to see their families?"

She gives the example that Sarah Schroeder, a recent mechanical engineering graduate, turned her back on job offers that required continuous sixty-hour work weeks and chose Saturn Corporation because of its "quality of work life" and "flexibility," in addition to the challenges of the job.

Many of the prospective recruits are "latch-key kids" of the Baby-Boomers who had little time with either of their parents as they grew up — and are determined not to have that happen to them. As the competition heats up, Shellenbarger says, more employers will need to respond to the change.

"Walk the Talk"

> *"Values are the gold that's in each of us.*
> *They're the real fortune of our organization."*
> **Eric Harvey and Alexander Lucia**
> **"Walk the Talk"**

Values aren't of any use unless we live by them. Living by what we believe in is living in integrity. That is no small task for a person or for an organization. According to Stephen Covey, 87 percent of business organizations in

America have a mission statement. They may even have it posted promi-
nently, perhaps on the wall of every office. But this doesn't necessarily mean
that the organization abides by the values it proclaims. Covey says the record
reflects that only 27 percent do so.[9]

Eric Harvey and Alexander Lucia have written a delightful fable about
honoring corporate values, a book entitled *Walk the Talk*, which tells the story
of a new CEO who is led through a visionary experience by a janitor named
Clarence.[10] While preparing his first speech to the company, which is strug-
gling financially, the CEO is led to the understanding that the corporate values and philosophies to which he was about to pay lip service are not, in fact,
the operating principles of the organization.

He discovers that the real fortune of the company is in its values, which
were built by the people who work there. He learns that those values have
been locked away, and that for the company to take advantage of its fortune,
it has to get them out and put them to use.

Without revealing the story further, I will just add that he also learns
about "corporate contradictions," such as the CEO and managers taking a
big bonus for keeping the company afloat while cutting back on everything
else. These contradictions between values and actions are practices that keep
the company from being able to use its fortune. Finally, he is led to see that
when a company *does* live by its values, good things happen.

Practicing your values, consciously factoring them into decision making and
policies, along with keeping your promises, doing what you say you will do, is
what the authors mean by *walking the talk*.

The New Elite

The systematic approach I have laid out for creating a great organization
is fairly simple in concept. It requires more human understanding than it
does technique. Most of all, it relies on *common sense* in dealing with people
and relationships.

These are the essential elements of building a great organization:

SELECT THE RIGHT PEOPLE

Choose people carefully. Make sure their values are compatible with your
corporate culture. Train them, nourish and encourage them, and then let
them take off on their own.

DEFINE MEANINGFUL VALUES AND MISSION

Get everyone involved in defining the meaning and purpose of the organization. Help everyone "own" the mission. Keep your values current and live by them.

PLAN STRATEGICALLY AND TACTICALLY

Involve the entire organization in the planning process. Identify the Big Picture and plan backward from it, establishing goals and objectives with the direct participation of the people who will carry out the tasks. Complete the entire planning cycle at least once a year.

CREATE A STRONG AND POSITIVE CORPORATE CULTURE

By honoring people and building trust in relationships, establish a work atmosphere that encourages people to care and engage their hearts as well as their minds. These are the conditions in which spirit can soar.

BUILD EFFECTIVE TEAMS

Create balanced teams for a well-rounded approach and try to get people in the right slots where they can play to their strong suits. Practice internal and external linking skills, especially listening and communicating. Use instruments such as the Team Management System and Myers-Briggs to reinforce teamwork and understanding, and the TAIS/ACT combination to enhance performance.

ACHIEVE VALUE-DRIVEN ALIGNMENT

Foster a relationship of cooperation and mutual trust among people. Create an organization that performs harmoniously, but with creative conflict.

HAVE FUN

Bring a healthy sense of humor into the workplace. Encourage people to laugh and have fun. Remember that laughter contributes to anyone's physical and mental well-being.

PROVIDE INSPIRING LEADERSHIP

No matter what else you do well, if you don't have solid leadership somewhere along the line, you're not going anywhere. Leadership is in caring for people and in earning trust. It is a matter of basic character and integrity. Look within yourself.

EXECUTE DILIGENTLY
Be diligent, on a day-to-day basis, in carrying out the tasks of the organization. Make plans happen for the organization and for individuals.

ALWAYS LOOK FOR A BETTER WAY OF DOING THINGS
Continue, ever and ever, to improve. Encourage innovation and flexibility.

The kind of organization we have been describing in this book — grounded in a rock-solid value base; honoring its people and releasing their full potential; operating with flexibility, innovation, and creativity — is what we might call *"The New Elite."* This kind of organization, as long as it maintains its focus and direction, will continue to produce at a peak level. Always, it is characterized by a mighty spirit, an indomitable *esprit de corps*.

These are companies that have the internal resources to deal with change. They are what Peter Senge, an authority on systems development, calls "learning organizations." They have the ability to constantly reinvent and recreate themselves in order to stay on the leading edge of competition. They are efficient because they use their most valuable resource, people, effectively. Achieving the alignment of values, mission, and goals among all members of the organization is a means of doing more with less. With the wholehearted support of their people, these organizations have infinitely more resources to draw upon. They harness the power of the human spirit.

ACKNOWLEDGEMENTS

As do the directors of many fine films, I have chosen to run credits at the end of this production. FLYING SPIRIT owes much to many. Good books, like good movies, are the products of many hands, hearts, and minds working together.

To Marilyn, my wife and partner in all things, words cannot adequately convey my appreciation and gratitude. We have been working together for the past twenty-five years to develop, apply, and continuously adapt my Air Force learning experiences to the world of organizations in both the private and the public sectors. Marilyn, you're one of a kind!

To my four sons, Steve, Mike, Dave and Will, who are the joys of my life, and my primary legacy to the world, my heartfelt thanks for your insights and support. In particular, in the case of this book, Mike and Will taught me more than I can measure as they helped streamline and apply our approach to leadership and management over the past eight years through the exceptionally dynamic growth of their company, Strategic Technologies, Inc., in Cary, North Carolina. I'd also like to acknowledge Marilyn's, and now my, gifted son, Jeff.

Two men without whom this book would have gone nowhere are Allen Overmyer, my partner and coauthor —an insightful writer with whom I forged a special bonding as I relived all the experiences I relate in FLYING SPIRIT — and Patrick Grace of Grace Associates, Ltd., with his uncanny talent for literary architecture. I also had the pleasure of watching the benefits brought to this book by Mark Phillips, a versatile graphic designer, and by Robert Adamich, a book production specialist.

Next, my hat is off to "a group of five," each a ground-breaking genius in his own right. Each contributed significantly to my understanding of people and organizations: Dr. Bob Nideffer, pioneer in human performance measurement and enhancement, working with world-class athletes and executives, who so graciously agreed to write the foreword; Dr. Bill Reckmeyer, leading-edge systems thinker and master of translating theory into practical approaches; Eric Sterling, a bright, articulate attorney and a shaker of a high order, who said, "What you and Marilyn really do is organize spirit," hence our title; Big Al Stark, senior Rubbermaid executive who taught me "all about strategy;" Win Wenger, a Mensa leader whose whole-brain approach ("Brain-Power Boosters") is state of the art.

Among the top leaders and "gurus" whom I have learned from either one-to-one or in seminars, and who all have helped to shape my approach, I want to cite: Ichak Adizes, Ken Blanchard, Richard Bolles, Stephen Covey, and Charles Garfield; , John Naisbitt, Curtiss Peck, Donald Petersen, Peter Senge, and Mike Vance. I also appreciate the counsel of a special friend, Steve Goldman.

Special thanks to those from client firms whose "write-in" pieces gave power and credibility to our models and processes, as described in the book: Pat Allen, Marty Berger, Jim Cain, Ben Clark, Rhett Linke, Pete Kauffman, Jeanetta Manuel, Robert Parrott, Neila Smith and Terry Stoneman.

My gratitude goes also to those who reviewed and commented upon one or more of the many versions of our book: Lt. Gen. B.O. Davis, Margaret Dunkle, Michael Gelb, Bonnie Gilewicz, Ron Guzik, Margaret Hartzler, Sig Hutchinson, Jay Levinson, Gen. Merrill A. McPeak, Ed Necco, Will Reed, Ron Tull, and my lifelong fighter-pilot mates and close friends: From Cross City, Florida, Monty Lennox, C.A. Smith, and Wild Bud Zeder; from the 506th Fighter Squadron, Harry Baker, Speedy Bealle, Ollie O. Simpson, my super crew chief, Pat Vercande, and our chief inspector, the late Lloyd (Lord) Shockey.

Last, but far from least, I want to acknowledge our clients over the years who hired Marilyn and me to teach them, but from whom both of us ended up learning so much, and with whom we forged so many wonderful friendships to name a few: from the U.S. Government, the Department of Agriculture, the Forest Service, the Departments of Health and Human Resources and Housing and Urban Development, the Internal Revenue Service, and the National Institutes of Health; from the private sector, a[4] Health Systems, Corning Besselaar, Federal Computer Systems, Holiday Corp., Hyatt Hotels, Interstate Johnson Lane, M.E.I. Software Systems, and the North Carolina Center for Nursing, as well as a host of individuals worldwide who attended our Life Management and Career Planning programs and our executive programs for Balancing and Blending Professional and Personal Lives.

NOTES

Chapter One — VALUING PEOPLE

1. John Naisbitt, *Trend Letter: The Global Network*, Vol. 13, No. 9, April 28, 1994.

2. Daniel Goleman, *Emotional Intelligence* (New York: Bantam Books, 1995), 34, referencing Howard Gardner, "Cracking Open the IQ Box," The American Prospect, Winter 1995.

3. Kenneth Blanchard and Spencer Johnson, *The One Minute Manager* (New York: Berkeley Books, 1983), 37.

4. Donald E. Petersen and John Hilkirk, *A Better Idea* (Boston: Houghton Mifflin Company, 1991), xiii.

Chapter Two — VALUES AND MISSION

1. Heraclitus, from Diogenes Laertius, *Lives of Eminent Philosophers*, bk. IX, sec. 8, and Plato, *Cratylus*, 402A.

2. Newton P. Stallknecht and Robert S. Brumbaugh, *The Spirit of Western Philosophy* (New York: Longmans, Green and Co., 1950), 150.

3. Huston Smith, *The Religions of Man* (New York: Harper & Row, 1986) 105.

4. Ibid., 150.

5. Ibid., 245.

6. John W. Gardner, *On Leadership* (New York: Free Press, 1990), 13.

7. Thomas A. Stewart, "Why Value Statements Don't Work," *Fortune Adviser 1997* (New York: Fortune Books, 1997), 104-109.

8. Mike Vance, *Think Out Of the Box* (Franklin Lakes, NJ: Career Press, 1995), 30.

9. Margaret J. Wheatley, *Leadership and the New Science* (San Francisco: Berrett-Koehler Publishers, Inc., 1992), 54.

10. Viktor E. Frankl, *Man's Search for Meaning* (New York: Simon & Schuster, 1959), 75-76.

11. Dr. Charles A. Garfield, *Peak Performers: The New Heroes of American Business* (New York: Avon Books, 1986), 24.

Chapter Three — PLANNING

1. Rick Atkinson, *The Washington Post*, May 29, 1994, A43.

2. Alfred P. Sloan, Jr., *My Years With General Motors* (Garden City, NY: Doubleday, 1963).

3. Dr. Edward C. Banfield, *The Unheavenly City, The Nature and Future of Our Urban Crisis* (Boston: Little, Brown, 1970).

4. Dr. Ichak Adizes, *The Pursuit of Prime* (Santa Monica, CA: Knowledge Exchange, LLC, 1996), 21-22.

5. Quoted in Vance, *Think*, 61.

6. Gary Hamel and C.K. Prahalad, *Competing for the Future* (Boston: Harvard Business School Press, 1994), 133-136.

Chapter Four — CREATIVITY

1. Dr. Willis Harman, Institute of Noetic Sciences, 475 Gate Five Road, Suite 300, P.O. Box 909, Sausalito, CA 94966-9922; Audiotape.

2. Ibid.

3. Dr. James Conner, "The Chemistry of Belief," *MORE... News from the Continuing Education Services Sector*, Volume IV, No. 1, Fall 1986.

4. Garfield, *Peak*, 160.

Chapter Five — THE ORGANIZING SPIRIT

1. James M. Kouzes and Barry Z. Posner, *The Leadership Challenge* (San Francisco: Jossey-Bass, 1995). 215-216.

2. Benjamin O. Davis, Jr., *Benjamin O. Davis, Jr., American* (Washington: Smithsonian Institution Press, 1991).

Chapter Six — BALANCE IN TEAM BUILDING

1. Dick McCann and Charles Margerison, "Managing High Performance Teams," *Training & Development Journal* (November 1989). American Society for Training and Development, Alexandria, Virginia. The Team Management Systems information, including the "Types of Work" model, the Team Management Wheel, and the Linking Skills Jigsaw, is used with permission of the authors. For more information on Team Management Systems, contact: Team Management Systems, 11718 Bowman Green Drive, Reston, VA 20190.

2. Warren Bennis, *Why Leaders Can't Lead* (San Francisco: Jossey-Bass Publishers, 1989), 108.

Chapter Seven — LINKING IN TEAMS

1. Charles Margerison, Dick McCann and Curtiss Peck, *Guide to Linking Within and Between Teams*, New Berlin, Wisconsin, National Consulting and Training Institute, 1990. Discussion of the "Eleven Skills of Linking" is drawn from Margerison, McCann and Peck and used with the authors' permission.

2. Goleman, *Emotional*, 161-163.

3. Vance, *Think*, 49.

4. Vance, *Think*, 67.

Chapter Eight — REINFORCING TEAMWORK

1. Peter F. Drucker, "The Age of Social Transformation," *The Atlantic Monthly* November 1994).

2. Bennis, *Why Leaders*, 92.

3. Ichak Adizes, Inc. 500 Conference, Los Angeles, California, June 13-15, 1996.

4. For further information on Myers-Briggs, see:

Sandra Krebs Hirsh, *Work It Out: Clues for Solving People Problems at Work* (Palo Alto, CA: Davies-Black Publishing, 1996).

Sandra Krebs Hirsch, *Using the Myers-Briggs Type Indicator® in Organizations* (2nd Ed.) (Palo Alto, CA: Consulting Psychologists Press, Inc., 1991).

David Keirsey and Marilyn Bates, *Please Understand Me: Character and Temperament Types* (Del Mar, CA: Prometheus Nemesis Book Company, 1984).

5. Hirsch, *Work It Out*, 21-22.

6. Ben Roach, "Organizational Decision Makers: Different Types for Different Levels," *Journal of Psychological Type* (1986), Volume 12.

7. Frederick F. Reichheld, *The Loyalty Effect* (Boston: Harvard Business School Press, 1996).

Chapter Nine — ALIGNMENT

1. Stephen R. Covey, *The Seven Habits of Highly Effective People* (New York: Simon & Schuster, 1989), 185-203.

2. U.S. Department of Defense, Joint Warfare of the U.S. Armed Forces.

3. Adizes, *Pursuit*, 22.

4. *The Washington Post*, January 1, 1993, C4.

5. Goleman, *Emotional*, 159-163.

Chapter Ten — FUN AND ENJOYMENT

1. Robert Ornstein, Ph.D., and David Sobel, M.D., *Healthy Pleasures* (Reading, MA: Addison-Wesley Publishing Company, Inc., 1989), 218.

2. Robert J. Kriegel and Louis Patler, *If It Ain't Broke... BREAK IT!* (New York: Warner Books, Inc., 1991), xvi-xvii.

Chapter Eleven — LEADERSHIP

1. Gardner, *On Leadership*, 51-52.

2. Bennis, *Why Leaders*, 21.

3. Gardner, *On Leadership*, 194.

4. Frankl, *Man's Search*, 105.

5. Mike Vance, at a private workshop for a corporation, August 14, 1994, Pinehurst, North Carolina.

6. Kouzes and Posner, *Leadership*, 8-14.

7. Ibid., 336.

8. Bennis, *Why Leaders*, 18.

9. Dr. Kenneth H. Blanchard, Blanchard Training and Development, Inc., 125 State Place, Escondido, California, 92029. Situational Leadership II materials used with the author's permission.

Chapter Twelve — EXECUTION: THE ART AND SCIENCE OF MAKING IT HAPPEN

1. Ronald E. Guzik, "In Business as in Nature — Everything is Connected!," *Svoboda's Business Magazine*, (March 1996).

2. Ibid.

Chapter Thirteen — THE RESTLESS QUEST FOR CONTINUING IM-PROVEMENT

1. Jane Hairston Romani, "Winning Strategies," *Business Leader*, Research Triangle Region, North Carolina, Volume 6, No. 12, (June 1995).

2. Dr. Robert M. Nideffer and Dr. Robin W. Pratt, Enhanced Performance Systems, P.O. Box 67197, 822 Boylston St., Chestnut Hill, Massachusetts 02167.

3. Covey, *Seven Habits*, 287.

4. Dr. Win Wenger and Richard Poe, *The Einstein Factor* (Rocklin, CA: Prima Publishing, 1996), 58-63.

5. Donald E. Petersen, correspondence, March 23, 1998.

6. Petersen and Hilkirk, *Better Idea*, 13.

7. Ibid., 21.

8. Ibid., 161.

9. Ibid., 13.

10. Ibid., 25.

Chapter Fourteen — HOLDING ON TO SUCCESS

1. Adizes, *Pursuit*, 8.

2. Dr. James Dobson, *The New Dare to Discipline* (Wheaton, IL: Tyndale House Publishers, Inc., 1992).

3. Vance, *Think*, 103-109.

4. George Gendron, "Flashes of Genius," State of Small Business, (special issue, *Inc. Magazine*, 1996), 30-43.

5. Kriegel and Patler, *If It Ain't Broke*, 1-9.

6. Curtiss Peck, Assessment Systems International, Inc., 15350 W. National Avenue, Suite 205, New Berlin, Wisconsin 53151-5158.

7. Betsy Morris, "Is Your Family Wrecking Your Career? (and vice versa)," *Fortune Magazine* (March 17, 1997).

8. Sue Shellenbarger, "New Job Hunters Ask Recruiters, 'Is There A Life After Work?'," *The Wall Street Journal* (January 29, 1997).

9. Stephen R. Covey, 11th Annual Conference, Entrepreneur of the Year Institute, Palm Springs, California, November 20-23, 1997.

10. Eric L. Harvey and Alexander D. Lucia, *Walk the Talk... And Get the Results You Want* (Dallas, TX: Executive Excellence, Inc., 1993).

INDEX

ABOUT THE AUTHORS

Hal Shook has proven his organization-building genius in the phenomenal success of a number of people-centered, highly spirited organizations. His methods have turned one startup company into an industry leader in computer technology services, with a 55 percent annual growth rate over ten years ($60 million-plus annual revenues in 1997). A pioneer in life management and career planning, Hal is president and cofounder, with his wife Marilyn, of Life Management Services, LLC, a consulting firm concentrated in the greater Washington, D.C., area and North Carolina. He graduated from the University of California, Berkeley, and holds graduate degrees from George Washington University and the National War College. He first learned his core leadership principles as the commander of a World War II fighter squadron before, during, and after the D-Day landing. He later commanded Air Force units numbering 300 (fighter squadron) to 5000 (air division) people.

The 506th Fighter Squadron Combat History of October 1944 said of him: *"Maj. Shook was, in the opinion of the men who flew with him and other officers and men in the squadron, the finest Commanding Officer they had ever been associated with. Without a doubt the finest fighter pilot, best navigator and all-around leader, he was tops as a C.O. In "Shooky" the pilots had an ideal leader they would follow anywhere. All officers and enlisted men exerted special effort because Shook wished something done and not because he ordered it done."*

During his command of the 506th, Hal Shook was awarded the Distinguished Flying Cross, the Air Medal with 19 Oak Leaf clusters, a Presidential Unit Citation, the Belgian Croix De Guerre, the French Croix De Guerre with Palm, and the Belgian Fourregère. He also holds the Commendation Medal with cluster and the Legion of Merit. He flew 105 combat missions.

Allen Overmyer is a former Foreign Service Officer with the U.S. Department of State. Among his assignments, he served in Israel during the 1973 war and as a political advisor to the Supreme Allied Commander at the NATO military headquarters in Belgium. As a consultant he recently developed a telecommunications management training program for China, under the auspices of the 18-nation community, Asia Pacific Economic Cooperation. He graduated from Yale and holds graduate degrees in journalism from Northwestern and in comparative literature from the University of Maryland. He is co-author of *Congress in Action* and lives in Arlington, Virginia, with his wife, Adele, and a gazelle-like Springer Spaniel.

LIFE MANAGEMENT SERVICES

Life Management Services (LMS), was co-founded by Hal and Marilyn Shook in 1976. LMS provides consulting services, workshops, counseling, and "train the trainer" programs in the areas of team building — strategic and tactical planning — leadership — life management and career planning.

As in FLYING SPIRIT, LMS provides a step-by-step approach that begins with recognizing people as the primary resource, lays a foundation of solid inner-core values, establishes vision, mission, and goals from those values and then brings everything together in the synergism of teamwork. The objective is to create an organization with the *esprit de corps* of a first-rate combat fighter squadron.

Hal and Marilyn welcome your comments on this book, and your inquiries:

301 Gregson Drive
Cary, North Carolina 27511
Phone: (919) 481-4707
Fax: (919) 469-4751
E-mail: shooklms@aol.com